THE SMART APPROACH TO
BATH DESIGN

THE SMART APPROACH TO
BATH
DESIGN

by Susan Maney

CREATIVE HOMEOWNER®, Upper Saddle River, New Jersey

Editorial Director: Timothy O. Bakke
Art Director: Annie Jeon

Editor: Kathie Robitz
Associate Editor: Lynn Elliott
Copy Editor: Laura Alavosus
Indexer: Sandi Schroeder

Graphic Designers: Jan H. Greco, Monduane Harris
Illustrator: Vincent Alessi

Cover and Book Design Concept: Annie Jeon
Cover Photography: Nancy Hill

Printed in the United States of America

Current Printing (last digit)
10 9 8 7 6

The Smart Approach To Bath Design
Library of Congress Catalog Card Number: 97-75267
ISBN: 1-58011-009-6

CREATIVE HOMEOWNER®
A Division of Federal Marketing Corp.
24 Park Way
Upper Saddle River, NJ 07458
Web site: **www.creativehomeowner.com**

DEDICATION

This book is dedicated to the best storyteller I know—my father. He inspired me to become a writer, and also taught me more about remodeling than he will ever know. Thanks, Dad. I also dedicate this book to my mother, who always encouraged me to capture my thoughts on paper. It's down on paper, now, Mom. Thank you both for everything.

ACKNOWLEDGMENTS

Thank you to all the people who shared their knowledge and encouragement. I especially want to thank my sister, Melissa, for her daily phone calls to see how the manuscript was coming; my brother, Mark, for his support; my best friend, Julie Peacock, for her unflagging encouragement and help; and my wonderful editor, Kathie Robitz, for her guidance and advice. A special thank you goes to the staff and members of the National Association of the Remodeling Industry (NARI) for sharing your knowledge, especially Bill Carmichael; Chris Miles; Jack Philbin, CR; Jonas Canemark, CR; David Tyson, CR; and Carol Winn—my best sources. Thank you to all the people I have interviewed about home remodeling in the last few years. A special acknowledgment goes to all those readers who relish a long, hot soak at the end of a long day. This book was written for you.

C O N T E N T S

INTRODUCTION

I have had a good many more uplifting thoughts, creative and expansive visions—while soaking in comfortable baths or drying myself after bracing showers—in well-equipped American bathrooms than I have ever had in any cathedral," said the twentieth-century literary critic and author Edmund Wilson.

That was his observation over 40 years ago. How Mr. Wilson would marvel at the innovations that characterize today's bathrooms, such as sumptuous oversized tubs and steam-equipped showers appointed with massaging water jets and multiple sprayers. With *The Smart Approach to Bath Design*, you'll learn how to incorporate them and others into your own plans.

Given the sophistication of the technology, it's hard to believe that the indoor bathroom is such a recent addition to the home. Even though Queen Elizabeth I boasted of bathing *once a month* in her sixteenth-century valve water closet—whether she needed it or not—indoor plumbing, in the form of a tub and toilet, has only been available to the average homeowner since the latter part of the nineteenth century.

Today, at least two and a half bathrooms are standard in new construction. For families still faced with the inconvenience of sharing one bathroom, imagine a time when families shared the same tub of water! It wasn't so long ago that water first had to be hand-pumped, then carried to the stove for heating before it was ready to be poured into a tub. Father, the head of the household, was the first to bathe, followed by each of the children, then, finally, Mother.

In his 1942 poem, *The Sense of the Sleight-of-Hand Man*, Wallace Stevens wrote, "One's grand flights, one's Sunday baths." Indeed, bathing should be an *indulgent escape*, not just a perfunctory hygienic task. But we are not the first generation to enjoy a therapeutic soak in the tub. Luxurious baths were commonplace centuries ago, with one difference: They were public spaces, not the private ones to which we are accustomed.

Although the private bath is a relatively modern concept, bathing in sumptuous surroundings is not. As early as the Minoan and the Roman civilizations, the bathhouse was a retreat from the pressures of everyday life, a place of renewal for the body and spirit. Early civilizations combined a variety of features in their bathhouses, but most typically, they consisted of steam chambers, dry heat rooms, and hot and cold tubs with water brought in via terra cotta pipes or aqueducts. The rooms were often opulently decorated with mosaics, paintings, statues, and intricate architectural details.

Bathing was elevated to an art, and in the process, bathhouses became centers of social activity. In the Roman city of Herculaneum, for instance, the bathhouse included a gymnasium and courts for ball playing; most people went to the baths daily. As the Roman Empire spread to the East, its bathing customs merged with those of the Byzantines and other nomadic people of the area. From that blending of cultures, the "Turkish bath" developed. Bathhouses featured cold and warm baths clustered around a steam chamber, and the experience involved relaxing in a saunalike room, followed by washing, massage, and cooling down.

After the fall of Rome, the use of public bathhouses declined throughout Europe until the eleventh and twelfth centuries. As new cities formed, the ritual of the public bath resurged. Some people also bathed at home in portable wooden tubs filled with heated water, but no real improvements were to come for centuries.

Finally in the late nineteenth century, the bathroom became a permanent, separate room in the home thanks to new developments in technology. Indoor plumbing became more commonplace and people became more conscious of hygiene. Not exactly sure how to decorate the bathroom, the Victorians kept the room functional. Vanities were made to look like pieces of furniture and claw-foot tubs abounded. They were favored for their easy access to the plumbing, which was unreliable.

By the 1920s, the bathroom was a gleaming monument to efficiency. The closed-in, porcelainized tub had replaced the claw-foot version, and the streamlined look of the pedestal sink made furniturelike vanities outdated. Truly luxurious bathrooms of this period featured separate, built-in showers instead of shower-bath combinations. The biggest news in the bathroom was *color*. White and bisque were still favorites for fixtures, but porcelain could be tinted in pastels, navy blue, or red. Although more stylish, the bathroom was still viewed as functional, not as a haven of relaxation.

Today, the bathroom has come full circle. Over the past couple of decades, the American bathroom has evolved from purely a necessary room to an at-home retreat for pampering oneself luxuriously. It is an amalgam of twenty-first-century technology and Old World refinement. Taking its cue from the centuries-old spas of Europe, the modern bath incorporates features that have been engineered to enhance relaxation and please the senses. And while doing so, good old Yankee ingenuity has made this room safer and more efficient to use, as well as handsome to look at in any price range.

If you are contemplating remodeling an old bathroom or building one that is entirely new, the most important element in creating your perfect retreat is the design. You may be considering hiring a team of professionals to take your desires from drawing table to reality. Or you may be contemplating doing some of the planning—and perhaps some of the construction—yourself. Either way, you can and should be an active participant in the design phase. For this truly personal space, your understanding and input is crucial to the final outcome.

The Smart Approach to Bath Design will help you with all of the aspects of your project. It will give you the confidence to make important decisions about working with professionals, developing a budget, rearranging space, developing a lighting plan, shopping for products, and decorating. It will help you analyze and organize your project just like a designer, walking you through all the steps that are necessary to bring your ideas to fruition. The easy-to-follow Smart Steps will take all the guesswork out of how to begin each phase of the process and what to do next.

The Smart Approach To Bath Design also will show you how to rely on your intuition and lifestyle as well as the traditional rules of function and design. You cannot ignore the physics of plumbing or the basics of electricity, but you can and should hold your own needs and requirements above what is typical. While you will need convenient storage, adequate ventilation, and a well-considered floor plan, you'll have to contemplate *your* individual requirements for the

ich as creating separate compartments for the
, tub, and toilet, or incorporating a mini greenhouse or an audio-video center. Today, anything goes.

This book will help you assess your current bathroom
and identify problem areas. It will delve into safety issues and possible future needs. You will discover the
basics of design and master ways to include the bath
into your home decor. But most importantly, you will
find out how to listen to yourself and plan a space that
can lull you into a stress-free state at the end of the day
or perk you right into action in the morning. *The Smart
Approach To Bath Design* will help you approach bath
design in the smartest way possible—personally. ❦

CHAPTER 1

THE BIG PICTURE

If the photographs in this book give you something to dream about, this chapter will give you lots to think about before you ever look at a paint chip or a tile sample. You may believe that true contentment comes with a new bathroom in which you can pamper yourself shamelessly. And it may. But the road to making that delightful fantasy come true is full of important decisions about who will actually do the work and what it will cost. It's fine to window shop, comb through books and magazines filled with beautiful pictures, and make lists of all the things you want your new bathroom to be, but come down to earth for a while and take stock of the big picture. Ultimately, this kind of planning is what can make or break the successful outcome of your remodeling endeavors.

Committing to a project of this size can be intimidating and exciting simultaneously. It is a major investment of time and money. But don't let your enthusiasm or any doubts cloud

Previous page: *A large-scale project like a restored bath or an addition typically requires architectural services.*
Left: *The owner of this new bath relied on the expertise of a certified bath designer to transform the space, which was formerly an extra bedroom.*
Right: *An interior designer gave this older bathroom a fresh face by suggesting new fixtures, tile, a window treatment, and other accessories.*

your objectives. One way to remain clear and keep from feeling overwhelmed is to avoid thinking about everything at the same time. Take it easy, and slow down. Do a little homework. Consider all your options regarding who will be involved in the bathroom project and how you will pay for it, *one step at a time.*

SMART STEPS

ONE: *Get the right help.* Redesigning and remodeling a bathroom requires skill and knowledge. In many cases, you will need to seek professional help at some point in the project, depending on your particular level of skill. But who

Above: *Review a designer's portfolio to see whether his or her "signature" style suits your taste. Old World ambiance is captured in this design.*
Left: *Clean geometric shapes streamline this contemporary bath.*

should you use? There are a number of professionals who can assist you. Here is a short list of those who would be qualified to offer advice.

❦ Architects. If you are planning a significant structural change in your bathroom, an architect is the best choice. While all licensed architects are schooled in design for both commercial and residential environments, one who regularly designs baths for one or two people to use versus those for thirty people is the best candidate for your project. The letters AIA after an architect's name indicates membership in the American Institute of Architects, a national association with local and state chapters that can offer referral services to consumers.

❦ Certified Bath Designers. Called CBDs, these trained people are certified by the National Kitchen & Bath Association as competent professionals who deal specifically in bath design and remodeling. Because they are specialists, they know the latest in bath products and trends and can help you choose the best layout and materials for your particular job. (Certified Kitchen Designers—or CKDs— often design bathrooms as well as kitchens and will have them on display in their showrooms.)

❦ Interior Designers. Interior designers can help you create style in your new bath and integrate it into the over-all look of your home. They do not make structural changes but work with color, pattern, and furnishings to shape a design. You may want to contact an interior designer if you are making significant cosmetic changes to your bath. Some states require licensing by the American Society of Interior Designers (ASID).

❦ Design-Build Remodeling Firms. These firms retain both designers and remodelers on staff. They are one-stop shops for

design help and construction. They are extremely popular because of the convenience of having all the necessary services within one company. If something goes wrong, you only have to make one call. There is no passing the buck here.

Below: *A custom-designed bathroom is a high-ticket item. Make sure you can afford it before plunging in.*

❧ Remodeling Contractors. Some contractors offer design as part of their remodeling services, or they partner with a design professional. A contractor is a good choice if you have already hired an architect to design the bath or if you are not changing the structure of your bath substantially. Always work with a licensed contractor.

Whenever you hire people to work in your home, first take the time to research them carefully. Your home is likely your largest single asset. Don't take chances with it unnecessarily. Interview professionals, and follow up on their references. Ask tough questions. Call state agencies and trade associations to check credentials.

Whomever you choose to help remodel the bath will end up knowing you and your family better than your lawyer or doctor. He or she will see you first thing in the morning and after a hard day at the office. That person will be a part of your family for the length of time it takes to complete the project. Check out all professionals as closely as you would a tenant in your home. In addition to getting professional help, take advice from books and magazines. Talk with friends and neighbors who have been through the process. The best approach is education. Clip out articles and photographs, collect notes and ideas, and hit the internet and television shows for further inspiration. Take all these tidbits of advice and ideas and put them in one place—a dream book or a drawer or even an idea box. This is the fun part of remodeling, when you can fantasize and start making wish lists of all those design elements and amenities you have coveted for years. That is, until your feet hit the ground and you wake up to the reality of *money*.

TWO: *Establish a working budget.* This is the not-so-fun part—finding the money. No one really likes to crunch numbers. Unfortunately, establishing a budget is the only way to determine the size and scope of the project you can afford to design. It is altogether disappointing to plan a luxurious bath complete with dra-

Left: *It took various subcontractors to finish this bath. If yours will require an electrician, a plumber, a tile setter, and others, get a lien waver for each one.*
Opposite: *This solid-surface countertop required special installation skills. Ask your contractor for a warranty on workmanship, besides materials.*

Smart Tips About Financing

Any bank or lending institution will be happy to tell you how much you can afford to spend on your home-remodeling project. But if you feel more comfortable running a test on your own, here is a quick and easy-to-understand overview of how banks figure out what you can spend.

The debt-to-income (DTI) ratio

This tells a lender if you can handle more debt on your current level of income. While each lender will have its own approved DTI, the average is normally at least 45 percent.

Current monthly expenses	$_____
Add the estimated monthly remodeling payment	+_____
Total expenses	$_____
Divide by your gross monthly income	÷_____
This is your DTI	_____%

How to find your maximum payment for remodeling

If your DTI doesn't qualify for financing options, you may need to lower the monthly remodeling expenditure. This calculation will show you how low you need to go.

Gross monthly income	$_____
Multiply by lender's DTI ratio	×_____
Subtotal	$_____
Subtract your total monthly expenses (not counting the estimated remodeling payment)	⁻_____
This gives you your maximum payment of	$_____

If the last line is negative, get ready to do the work yourself on a very tight budget. A negative number means you won't be receiving funds from a lender. On the other hand, you could check out other options that may help you fund this project. For example, consider a consolidation loan, which allows you to incorporate your current debts into the home-improvement loan. A consolidation loan does two things for you. First, it lowers the monthly cost of your current debts. Second, it allows you to deduct the interest on the loan from your taxes, something you can't do on other forms of debt.

You might also think about other forms of financing besides home equity loans. There are a variety of them in today's financial market. You could take out a loan against investments, borrow against your credit card, or the perennial favorite: a private loan from a family member.

matic fiber-optic lighting and a cozy fireplace only to find you can barely afford task lighting and a heated towel bar.

Try to avoid paying cash for remodeling. If it comes down to a choice between paying cash for remodeling or for buying a new car, always go the cash route for the car and finance the remodeling. You can deduct the interest of the remodeling loan from your taxes; you can't deduct the interest on a car loan. Unfortunately, many homeowners will gladly put money up front for a home-improvement project and finance the car. It doesn't make sense.

It also doesn't make sense to set aside money or sign a loan for $20,000 to $30,000 without preparing yourself. How much time would you spend investigating new cars before buying? You would probably read performance reports on various makes and models, then test drive several vehicles before finally making a purchase. Approach a home-improvement loan the same way. Take the time to investigate your financing options.

When seeking estimates from contractors, comparison shop. Use the plans and specifications for your new bathroom to shop with. If you can't draw them yourself, pay a designer to do it.

THREE: *Familiarize yourself with legal issues.* Anytime you enter into an agreement, you are venturing into the legal world of a litigious society. Luckily, as one of the contractual parties, you have certain rights. For example, you can change your mind. This is called the legal "Right of Recision." It allows you to change your mind within three days of signing the contract without any liability if the contract was obtained at some place other than the designer's or contractor's office—your home, for instance. This grace period protects you against hasty decisions and hard sells. Federal law mandates that consumers must be made aware of this right to cancel the contract without penalty. Ask your contractor about it before you sign anything.

You should also request waivers of lien, which release you from liabilities for subcontractors and manufacturers. At the end of the job, ask for a final lien waiver for each person who worked on the project to protect yourself from third-party debts and obligations. You don't want

Above: *Even a vintage bathroom that is refurbished and restored must adhere to updated building codes.*

to be forced, legally, into paying for a job twice because your general contractor didn't make good on his debts. With a lien waiver, you can refer an unpaid subcontractor to the general contractor for payment. For further protection, ask your contractor for a signed affidavit stating that all subcontractors have been paid.

Furthermore, don't allow anything to happen on your property that is not outlined in writing. If you want a change, get a written "change order." Remember, though, that any change—whether initiated by you or not—will cost more money. It is the nature of the game. Write up every change order with a description what is to be done and how much it will cost. Always include an estimate of how long the additional work will take to complete and how it will impact the production schedule and project timeline.

FOUR: *Review licenses, insurance, and permits.* Ask to see the remodeler's license, if your local or state government requires one. Call the licensing agent, and verify the status of the license. Just seeing one is not enough. Normally, expiration or suspension notices do not appear on the license itself. You have to call the licensing agency for that information.

All contractors should have current liability insurance and worker's compensation. This insurance covers employees of the remodeling firm while they are working on your property. Make sure your contractor carries this coverage before allowing uninsured workers to place themselves in potentially hazardous situations in and around your home. If you are still worried about your legal liabilities should an injury occur, talk to your insurance carrier and attorney. You may want your insurance agent to review the plans for the new bathroom and adjust your homeowner's coverage during the length of the project.

Smart Tips about Contracts

You have the right to a specific and binding contract. The more details and pages in it, the better. Get specifics for every part of the project and for every product purchased. It is the detail that will save you in the long run. Every contract should include some basic items, such as

- The contractor's name and proper company name, as listed on the business license

- The company address, telephone number, and fax number

- The company's remodeling license number if applicable (Some states don't require licensing. If this is the case, verify the company's business license.)

- Details of what the contractor will and will not do during the project, such as daily cleanup around the site, final cleanup, security measures that will be taken during the demolition, and so on

- A detailed list of all materials and products including size, color, model, brand name, and specific product (If you have it written down, it can't change without two signatures—yours and the contractor's.)

- The approximate start date and substantial completion dates (If you can, ask for estimated completion dates for the various stages.)

- Your signature required on all plans before work begins (This prevents last-minute changes without your knowledge. It also prevents any misunderstandings. You get a chance to look at the plans one last time before walls come down and tubs are installed in the wrong corner of the room. However, a drawback to this provision is that it could cause delays if you are out of town during the renovation or if you are slow to respond. In this case, you may want to provide an address where you can be reached by overnight carrier or designate someone to sign in your absence.)

- A detailed description of the financial terms, including total price, payment schedule, and any cancellation penalty (Don't be surprised if the contractor wants a fifty to sixty percent deposit to cover the cost of bath fixtures.)

- Procedures for handling changes in the scope of the work during the course of the project (The procedures should state how change orders will be handled by the contractor. Change orders should require both your signature and the contractor's.)

- A listing and full description of warranties covering materials and workmanship for the project (Warranties are normally for one year. Make sure yours is identified as either "full" or "limited." A "full" warranty covers full repair of faulty products, or replacement, or your money is returned. A "limited" warranty indicates that replacements and refunds of damaged products are limited in some regard. For example, it may cover replacement of only a part of a faucet.)

- A binding arbitration clause in the event of a disagreement (Arbitration enables both parties to resolve disputes quickly and effectively without litigation.)

- A provision for waivers of liens to be provided to you prior to making any payment

- Anything else you want spelled out clearly (If it isn't in writing, legally it does not exist. However, plans and specifications often take precedent over a written contract in court.)

Before signing any contract, be sure you understand all the components involved. You have the right to ask questions and to demand explanations. Never sign an incomplete contract.

Left: *Replacing the sink and counter-top was a weekend project.*

by, but after a tragedy such as fire happens, you can bet your insurance agency and fire marshal will investigate all the causes. When the cause is faulty electrical work that was done during your bath remodeling, your homeowner's insurance company can refuse to pay the claim if there is no permit on record. This could be disastrous should the entire house burn down.

FIVE: *Have it your way.* It's your house and your money. Don't hesitate to ask as many questions as you like about any detail concerning the project. The more information you have, the happier you will be with the result. This is particularly true when selecting products or figuring out warranty coverage. Find out what is and isn't covered by warranties. Many manufacturers won't honor a warranty if an amateur fix-it job has been attempted. Avoid disasters by calling your contractor or the manufacturer for guidance about repairs.

Never sign for any deliveries during a job unless you personally ordered the materials or are prepared to be liable for them. Signing for materials is your

Never allow work to be done on your home without a legal permit. Permits may require fees and inspections, but they could save you thousands of dollars in the future. In some states, you, the homeowner, are held responsible if work is done without a permit and a problem occurs. Years may go contractor's responsibility. Imagine what would happen if you signed for an incomplete shipment or the wrong-size floor tiles. You would be responsible for the error. Don't take chances. Let your contractor shoulder the burden of tracking down incomplete, incorrect, or damaged orders.

Also remember, the people you hire to work in your home are in your home. You have every right to tell them not to smoke, play music, curse, or eat inside. You can even tell them where to park and how to store tools and materials around your home. Of course, don't be unreasonable, but don't feel put out in your own home, either. Make a set of rules before the work begins, and ask the general contractor to enforce them. If he or she doesn't, do it yourself. It is a good idea to include your rules as part of the contract. That way, you'll have some legal ground to stand on when making your demands. In most cases, however, a reputable contractor will make sure workers are respectful of your wishes.

SIX: *Talk the talk.* Don't let miscommunication come between you and the person you hire. Learn how to make yourself understood. If you are going to remodel, get to know the construction language and jargon. Be sure to check out the glossary in the back of this book for a listing of commonly used terms in bath remodeling.

Decide how you are going to convey problems to your contractor. Again, if you know how you will respond should something go wrong, you won't panic. Are you someone who does not deal well with stress or confrontation? Perhaps someone else in the household could take over the day-to-day communication with the contractor—preferably someone who understands the basic process and can stay calm. Maybe your talents would be better spent in the early planning stages and the final decoration.

SEVEN: *Prepare yourself emotionally.* Remodeling is stressful. There is no way around it, even if you do the work yourself

Right: *In a bathroom like this one, glazing the walls would be a simple job for the relatively inexperienced do-it-yourselfer.*

Smart Tips About Permits

If your contractor tells you to obtain the permit yourself, refuse. While most jurisdictions require permits, they also hold the person who obtained the permit responsible for the outcome of the job. If you get the permit, you will be considered the general contractor. The county or building officials in your jurisdiction will come to you if the work is not up to code during the inspection. If these officials find a problem, it is far better to let them talk to a professional.

If you are doing the work yourself, find out the rules in your particular area. Some types of work require a licensed professional to meet code. Many jurisdictions, for example, won't accept amateur work on electrical systems because an error can cause severe physical damage to the house and cost lives. Don't gamble.

Regardless of whether you use a professional or not, get a copy of the permit and file it away for future reference. This will help prevent any problems down the road. It also helps you ensure a professional job—one done correctly and safely. Permits were created to make sure a job is completed to code, and there may be a safety reason behind that.

Left: *Installing wallpaper and a border added a lot of style to this bathroom, and it was a simple project for the homeowners.*
Opposite: *Putting in a large tub involved adding more structural support to the floor—a task not to be taken on by amateurs.*

(perhaps especially if you do the work yourself). It's hard to deal with the sawdust, the noise, and the constant inconvenience of not having a bathroom. At times it will seem as if the project is something that is being done to you rather than for you. But there are ways to ready yourself and your family for the temporary upheaval that could last just a few weeks or maybe months, depending upon how much actual work will be done.

Begin by talking to everyone in the family about what is involved. Discuss any temporary inconveniences all of you can expect and for how long. If there's only one bathroom in the house, you'll have to make plans to stay elsewhere for at least part of the time. Ask your contractor to give you enough warning. If there are going to be strangers in the house, let everyone meet them before the project begins. Your home is your most personal asset and your most private retreat. It is also essential that you and your family know how to protect it and yourselves before there are unfamiliar faces walking in and about your house for an extended period of time.

Contractors often talk about what they call the "remodeling curve"—the wave of ups and downs everyone involved in remodeling goes through. Some days are good (when you see the framing done) and some days are bad (you can't tell whether anything has happened in days). It is normal to experience highs and lows during a project of any size. What helps is to talk about it, expect it, and prepare for it. Decide ahead of time to order out Chinese food or take the kids to their favorite burger joint on those days when it feels as if nothing is going the way everybody would like. Find some way to stave off the frustration. You will feel more in control if you have a plan of action. (See Chapter Eight, "Remodeling Timeline at a Glance," page 158.)

EIGHT: *Evaluate your do-it-yourself skills.* Can you do a bath remodel? It depends. The National Association of the Remodeling Industry (NARI) offers a quiz to determine whether you should try it yourself or leave it to a pro. Take the test and see for yourself:

Yes No   Do you enjoy physical work?

Yes No   Are you persistent and patient? Do you have reliable work habits—meaning that once the project is started, it will get finished?

Yes No   Do you have all the tools needed and, more importantly, the skills required to do the job?

Yes No   What quality level do you need for this project? Are your skills at that level?

Yes No   Do you have the time that will be required to complete the project? (Always double or triple the time estimated for a DIY project, unless you are highly skilled and familiar with that type of work.)

Yes No   Will it matter if the project remains unfinished for a period of time?

Yes No   Are you prepared to handle the kind of stress this project will create in your family relationships?

Yes No   Have you performed all of the steps involved in the project before?

Yes No   Have you gotten the installation instructions from the manufacturers of the various products and fixtures to determine whether this is a project you still want to undertake? (Most manufacturers will send you installation instructions before purchase to determine whether the product will meet your needs. The instructions outline the steps involved in installation and can be an excellent guide to determine the skill level required to accomplish the job adequately.)

Yes No   Is this a job you can do completely by yourself or will you need assistance? If you need assistance, what skill level is involved for your assis-tant? If you need a professional subcontractor, do you have access to a skilled labor pool?

Yes No   Are you familiar with your local building codes and permit requirements? (Some jurisdictions require the work be completed by a licensed professional in order to meet code. Otherwise, the finished job may not pass inspection.)

Yes No   What will you do if the project goes awry? (Most contractors are wary about taking on a botched DIY job, and many just won't. The liability is too high.)

Yes No   Is it safe for you to do this project? (If you are unfamiliar with roofing [for a bath addition] or do not have fall protection restraints, you may not want to venture into a roofing job.

Opposite: *The trained eye of an architect is obvious in this unique bathroom addition, which features a dramatic domed ceiling and the artful application of materials.*
Right: *Skilled tradesman created the custom cabinetry and the stone countertop and flooring.*

Similarly, if you know nothing about electricity—leave it to the professionals. Some jobs can have fatal consequences if not performed correctly. Your health and safety should be the primary concern. Never enter into a DIY project that could jeopardize them.)

Yes No Will you be able to obtain the materials you need? Who will be your supplier?

Yes No Are you attempting to do it yourself for financial reasons? If so, have you looked at all your costs, including the cost of materials, your time, and the tools you need to purchase? If you are new to the DIY game, you may also want to look at the cost to correct any mistakes you may make—for example, the damage factor. Will it still be a cost-saving venture given all of these?

Yes No If you are trying DIY for the satisfaction of a job well done—can you ensure that the job will be "well done"? If it doesn't come out right, how will you feel? Can you afford to redo any unsatisfactory work? Will you be able to live with it as is?

NARI says if you marked a majority of the answers "yes," you may want to attempt doing it yourself. But before you strap on a carpenter's tool belt, revisit those questions you marked "no." Carefully consider the potential problems you will face in those areas if you proceed with the project. Hiring a professional may still be your best option. Or you may want to use a combination of the two—hiring a professional for the technical and difficult aspects of the job and doing the cosmetic touches yourself. Only you can decide.

For additional advice on whether to go to a professional or try it yourself, you can call the NARI Homeowner Remodeling Hotline at 1-800-440-NARI (6274) for a free copy of *The Master Plan for Professional Home Remodeling*, which provides additional tests and checklists.

The key is to be honest with yourself. Can you really do this project—or parts of this project—yourself? If so, wonderful. A successful do-it-yourself project can be quite satisfying. If not, then be smart and hire the right professional to help you out. Trade associations like NARI, the National Kitchen and Bath Association, American Institute of Architects, and others are great places to look for top-of-the-line advice.

Finally, if you plan to sell your house at any time, find out what kind of bathroom amenities buyers expect in your area. A local real estate agent can help you with that information. But whatever buyers want, bringing an existing bathroom up to date or adding the convenience of an extra one is always money well spent. If you do all of the work yourself, you'll probably recoup almost all of your investment. If you hire professionals, expect to get back about forty percent of what you paid.

Left: *A work-intensive project like this custom tub and shower may actually cost more—in labor hours—than if you hired a professional to do the job.*

What You'll Pay

The following information will help you put the costs of professional labor and materials for your new bath into perspective. A good portion of a contractor's fee is based on these two factors. If you plan to do much of the work yourself, expect to spend more time on a job than a skilled contractor. The National Association of the Remodeling

Industry recommends reserving 10 percent of your budget for any unforeseen or hidden expenses. If your house is more than a few years old, it may require certain upgrades to meet more recent codes. You may have to update the electrical or plumbing systems, for example. Don't be caught short by costs you never anticipated.

STANDARD HALF BATH (room size: 4x6 feet)

Description	Quantity/Unit	Labor-Hours	Materials
Rough-in frame for medicine cabinet, 2x4 stock	8 L.F.	0.3	$3.65
Flooring, underlayment-grade, hardboard, 3/16 inch thick, 4x4-foot sheets	32 S.F.	0.3	$15.74
Paint, ceiling, walls, door, primer, one coat	162 S.F.	0.6	$7.78
Medicine cabinet with mirror, 16x22 inches, unlighted	1	0.6	$74.40
Vanity cabinet, 30 inches wide	1	1.0	$150.00
Basic plastic laminate countertop	1	0.3	$5.87
Lavatory, with trim, porcelain enamel on cast iron, 18 inches around	1	2.5	$217.20
Lavatory fittings	1 set	7.0	$112.20
Towel bars, stainless steel, 18 inches long	1	0.4	$33.00
Toilet-tissue dispenser, surface-mounted, stainless steel	1	0.3	$11.52
Flooring, vinyl sheet goods, backed, 0.080 inch thick	20 S.F.	0.7	$35.52
Toilet, tank-type, vitreous china, floor-mounted, two-piece, white	1	3.0	$174.00
Toilet fittings	1 set	5.3	$145.20
Electrical, one light fixture with wiring	1	0.3	$42.00
Electrical, one light switch	1	1.4	$22.32
Electrical, one GFCI outlet	1	1.7	$53.40
Totals		25.7	$1,103.80

Key to abbreviations
S.F.- square feet
L.F. - linear feet

Contractor's fee, including materials: **$2,705**

What You'll Pay (continued)

STANDARD FULL BATH (room size: 7x8 feet)

Description	Quantity/ Unit	Labor-Hours	Materials
Partition wall, 2x4 plates and studs, 16 inches on center, 8 feet high	64 L.F.	0.9	$27.65
Drywall, 1/2 inch thick, water-resistant, taped and finished, 4x8-foot sheets	64 S.F.	1.1	$24.58
Paint, ceiling, walls, and door, primer	230 S.F.	0.9	$11.04
Paint, ceiling, walls, and door, one coat	230 S.F.	1.4	$11.04
Vanity base cabinet, deluxe, two-door, 30 inches wide	1	1.4	$216.72
Vanity top, solid surface material, with center bowl 17x19 inches	1	2.0	$777.00
Lavatory fittings	1 set	7.0	$88.80
Bathtub, recessed, porcelain enamel on cast iron, with trim, mat bottom, 5 feet long, color	1	3.6	$408.00
Fittings for tub and shower	1 set	7.7	$154.80
Sliding shower door, deluxe, tempered glass	1	1.0	$258.00
Mirror, plate glass, 30x34 inches	7 S.F.	0.7	$44.94
Walls, 4 1/4 x4 1/4-inch ceramic tile, shower enclosure and wainscoting, thin set	140 S.F.	11.8	$371.28
Flooring, porcelain tile, one color, 4 1/4 x4 1/4-inch tiles	36 S.F.	3.2	$300.24
Toilet, tank-type, vitreous china, floor-mounted, one-piece, color	1	3.9	$686.40
Toilet fittings	1 set	5.3	$139.20
Toilet-tissue dispenser, surface-mounted, stainless steel	1	0.3	$12.30
Towel bar, stainless steel, 30 inches long	1	0.4	$35.40
Electrical, two light fixtures with wiring	4	1.1	$168.00
Electrical, two light switches	2	2.8	$40.92
Electrical, one GFCI outlet	1	1.7	$52.20
Totals		58.2	$3,828.51

Key to abbreviations
S.F.- square feet
L.F. - linear feet

Contractor's fee, including materials: $7,997

DELUXE MASTER BATH (room size: 8x10 feet)

Description	Quantity/ Unit	Labor- Hours	Materials
Partition for shower stall, 2x4 plates and studs, 16 inches on center, 8 feet high	152 L.F.	2.2	$69.31
Drywall, 1/2 inch thick, water-resistant, taped and finished, 4x8-foot sheets	160 S.F.	2.7	$61.44
Paint, ceiling, walls, door, primer	330 S.F.	1.3	$15.84
Paint, ceiling, walls, door, one coat	330 S.F.	2.0	$15.84
Deluxe vanity base cabinet, two-door, 72 inches wide	1	1.7	$235.20
Lavatory, solid surface material with integral bowl, 22x73 inches	1	1.0	$858.00
Lavatory fittings	2 sets	13.9	$224.40
Shower stall, terrazzo receptor, 36x36 inches	1	8.0	$894.00
Shower door, tempered glass, deluxe	1	1.3	$241.20
Tub, recessed, porcelain enamel on cast iron, with trim, mat bottom, 5 feet long	1	3.6	$450.00
Fittings for tub	1 set	7.7	$163.20
Fittings for shower, thermostatic	1 set	1.0	$266.40
Inlet strainer for shower	1		$79.80
Walls, ceramic tile, stall and wainscoting, thin set, 4 1/2 x 4 1/2 inches	170 S.F.	14.3	$414.12
Flooring, porcelain tile, 1 color, color group 2, 2x2 inches	40 S.F.	3.4	$191.04
Toilet, tank-type, vitreous china, floor-mounted, one-piece, color	1	3.9	$678.60
Toilet fittings	1 set	5.3	$145.20
Towel bar, ceramic	4	0.8	$46.32
Toilet tissue dispenser, ceramic	1	0.2	$11.58
Electrical, light fixtures with wiring	4	1.1	$168.00
Electrical, two light switches	2	2.8	$44.64
Mirror, plate glass, 34 inches high x 60 inches wide	1	1.4	$80.64
Electrical, one GFCI outlet	1	1.7	$53.40
Ceiling light/fan/heat unit	1	0.8	$88.80
Totals		82.1	$5,496.97

Key to abbreviations
S.F.- square feet
L.F. - linear feet

Contractor's fee, including materials: $11,351

Reprinted with permission from *Interior Home Improvement Costs* (R.S. Means Co., 1998)

FUNCTION: UP CLOSE & PERSONAL

Professionals know that good design in any room of the house reflects the personalities and lifestyles of the people who live there. Later in this book, we'll discuss decorating issues, but you'll never be happy even with the most beautifully outfitted room if it is not functional and practical. A delicate handpainted sink may be a showpiece, but it needs tender loving care to keep it beautiful. If this kind of maintenance doesn't fit into the way you live, you'll regret the day you bought that sink. Design your bath to pamper *you*, not the other way around.

Architect Louis Sullivan said, "Form follows function." That does not mean that style has to be subservient to function, but there must be a balance between the two. So even if you have a clear picture about how you want the new bathroom to look, put that thought on hold—temporarily—and think about how it will work.

Don't mislead yourself into believing only a luxurious plan demands this kind of attention. Even if you are designing a modest bath you can greatly increase its performance and your ultimate comfort by thoughtfully planning out every square inch of floor and wall space.

Whatever the size of your investment, you should get the most out of it. Besides, if you ever decide to sell your house, potential buyers will be put off by cramped bathrooms that look like everything was designed as an

Previous page: *Twin sinks and separate bathing areas enhance the function of a master bath.*
Left: *An all-glass shower admits sunlight into this room.*
Opposite: *A wall of custom-built cabinetry and a double vanity makes room for two.*

afterthought. On the other hand, you can make a splash—and perhaps a tidy profit—if the fixtures are in good condition, the floor plan appears carefully thought out, the room looks bright, and there is ample storage.

DECIDING WHAT YOU NEED AND WANT

If you will be working with a design professional, expect to be interviewed at the beginning of the planning stage. He or she will want to get to know you and whoever else will use the new bathroom. Your designer isn't being nosy. He

or she simply wants to understand your likes and habits, as well as your basic requirements and greatest expectations with respect to the new bath. Your designer will also make a sketch of the existing space to get an idea of what works and what doesn't. The rough drawing may include any adjacent areas that might be considered for expansion, such as a closet or part of a hallway.

If you will be acting as your own designer, do the same. You can't assume that you instinctively know what has to be done to transform the old bathroom into a fabulous new space just because you live there. That's acting on emotion. For the best result, approach the project in the same analytical manner as a professional who understands design and can be objective about what has to happen.

SMART STEPS

ONE: *Create a design notebook.* It's important to keep all your ideas and records in one place. Buy a loose-leaf binder, and use it to organize everything from magazine clippings to photos of the old bathroom, wish lists, notes and interviews with design professionals, contracts, sample plans, shopping lists, color charts, tile samples, fabric and wallpaper samples, and anything else related to your project. It should be comprehensive yet not too clumsy to cart around to showrooms, stores, or home centers.

TWO: *Analyze the existing bathroom.* Before you start clipping too many photographs out of magazines, decide what you really want to gain by remodeling. You might begin by asking the most obvious question, "What's wrong with my existing bathroom?" You already know there's something you don't like about it. Maybe it's just old and outdated. Perhaps it's too small. To decide what you must do specifically to improve the bathroom, ask yourself the kinds of questions any design professional would pose to a client. Record your responses in your notebook.

Begin with, "Who uses this bath on a regular basis?" Jot down bathing preferences. If someone likes a shower

Left: *Access to a private garden and hot tub indulge the owners' desire for an at-home getaway.*
Above: *Pedestal sinks can be functional in vintage, as well as contemporary, settings. A cabinet and a wall ledge make up for the sinks' lack of surface storage.*

instead of a bath, he might prefer a separate unit, with amenities like jetted sprayers, to a whirlpool tub. If the design is part of a master suite, will partners bathe together? A large soaking tub for two may be in order.

Examine the condition of the fixtures. Will you replace all of them, some of them, or none of them? If they are in good condition, you can save money by simply refinishing them. Tradespeople who specialize in recoating enamel fixtures can be found easily in the Yellow Pages.

Does the existing bathroom contain enough storage space? Even if there is a linen closet or cabinetry in the room, it may not be organized efficiently. If you need more storage, make note of it now so that it can be planned as part of the total design.

Also ask yourself whether the fixtures are comfortably situated. Are the sink and toilet installed at the right height for the people who will be using the bathroom? Is the toilet paper dispenser handy? Are the controls easy to use? Are there enough towel racks? Are they easy to reach? There is no one standard prescribed for everybody, and now is the time to get things the way you want them to be.

A new bathroom is a substantial investment, even on a small scale, so don't overlook these less glamorous but important aspects of function.

You would be wise to think about maintenance, too. Do existing materials keep you busy with constant cleaning and polishing? A black tub may look sleek and sophisticated, for example, but it shows every streak of water. Do you want to keep polishing it, or is it worth the cost of replacing it with one that's white or beige?

Make sure to take safety matters into account in your analysis. For example, are there adequate Ground Fault Circuit Interrupters (GFCIs)? Ordinary receptacles can't protect you against the full force of an electrical shock. GFCIs sense an overload on the circuit and cut the current in a faction of a second. That's faster than your heart beats. Other safety questions to ask include: Is the existing flooring slippery? Is there a tub or shower seat in the bathing area? Can you reach the bath controls from both a sitting and standing position? In addition, the shower head should have a hand-held unit that is easy to use when sitting or when you're bathing children. And there should be a temperature- and surge-protection device installed with the faucet to prevent scalding.

Now is also the time to question whether the existing bathroom has enough heat and light. Is it well ventilated?

Finally, if you plan to stay in the house after retirement, evaluate the bathroom layout's potential for accommodating a wheelchair or walker. (See Chapter Three, "Safety and Universal Design.") Hopefully, you'll never need either one, but making the necessary changes later may be more than you can handle at that stage.

The answers to these questions should give you a detailed idea about what needs improvement and what may not. If you are adding a bath to the house, the list should alert you to details you don't want to overlook in its design.

THREE: *Make a wish list.* The design is right when it meets your personal needs and appeals to your senses. Everyone has different habits, individual ways of getting ready in the morning or winding down at night. In fact, some psychologists say that people's hygiene routines will determine how well they sleep and handle stress. If this is true, your bathroom actually may affect your well-being.

Besides basic elements, you may want some special features in your new bathroom. Create a list of all the amenities you would like to include, whether or not you think you can afford them. When you come up with a close-to-perfect plan, look for areas to trim expenses. The money you save may permit a few extras. Suggestions include choosing an affordable laminate countertop and less expensive cabinetry or tilework or keeping old fixtures that are in good condition.

Chapter Six, "Selecting Products and Materials," presents just about all of the bath options on the market, from basic to luxurious. As you compile your wish list, review that chapter, taking note of everything that fits into your fantasy of the perfect bathroom, in addition to practical features. To make sure your wish list is complete, visit bath design showrooms and home centers. Talk to salespeople who can tell you about new product introductions.

FOUR: *Sketch the old floor plan.* Just like the professional designer, make a drawing of the existing floor plan. First draw a *rough* sketch, and then transfer your drawing to graph paper with grids marked at ¹⁄₄-inch intervals. This formal drawing of the physical layout of the bathroom is called a "base map" or a "base plan." You can draw it freehand or with a straightedge, but do it to a scale of ¹⁄₂ inch equal to 1 foot.

Start by taking measurements, beginning with the length and width of the room. Then working from one corner, measure the location of all windows, doors, and walls. Record the swing of each door. Note each dimension in feet and inches to the nearest ¹⁄₄ inch. If the room is small and you have a good steel measuring tape, you may be able to make all the measurements by yourself, but it's always easier to have a helper hold the "dumb" end of the measuring tape.

Next, draw the cabinetry and plumbing fixtures, and indicate their heights. Measure the centerline of sinks, toilets, and bidets, and show how far the center of each of these

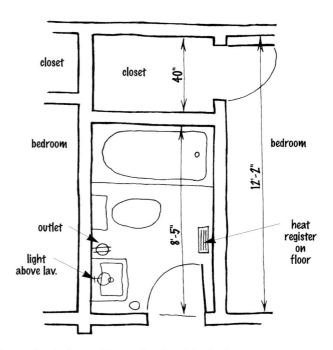

Above: *Begin by making a sketch of the bathroom as it now exists. Include any adjacent areas that might be used for expansion. Indicate fixtures and electrical and heating features.*
Below: *Use your rough sketch to create a base plan that is drawn to a scale of ¹⁄₂ inch to 1 foot.*

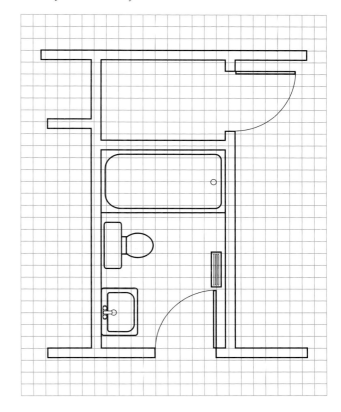

fixtures is from the wall. Be sure to list the overall lengths and widths. Unless the corners of the room are extremely out of square, or the walls are leaning, don't worry about small discrepancies in their measurements. Most houses are not perfect. Include symbols for light fixtures, outlets, and heat registers. Make notations for load-bearing walls if you can. Otherwise, consult a trained professional who can tell you whether a wall can be moved safely.

It's a good idea to list your gripes about the old bathroom right on this sketch. That way you can see exactly what you

want to change and what you want to keep at a glance. Remember, this map is simply your guide. It doesn't have to be professionally drawn, but it must be accurate in its rendition of the space as it is now to be useful.

CREATING FUNCTIONAL SPACE

Whether it's a full-size bath or a powder room, the arrangement of space plays a large role in how well the room will function. A bathroom addition to an outside wall of the house offers the best possibilities for unen-

Existing Bath

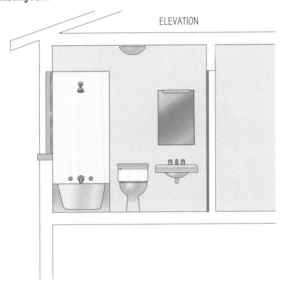

ELEVATION

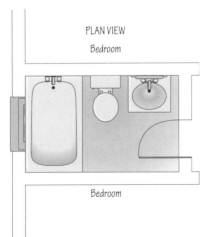

PLAN VIEW
Bedroom

Bedroom

Above: *This elevation and plan show a typical minimum-size full bath between two bedrooms.*

New Bath

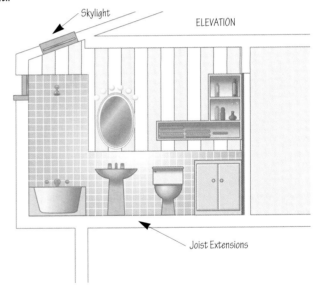

Skylight

ELEVATION

Joist Extensions

PLAN VIEW

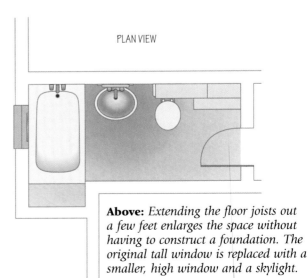

Above: *Extending the floor joists out a few feet enlarges the space without having to construct a foundation. The original tall window is replaced with a smaller, high window and a skylight.*

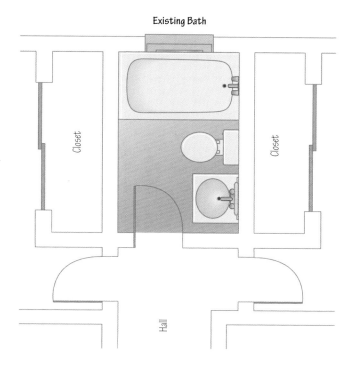

Existing Bath

Above: *This typical in-line full bath is situated between two bedrooms. Large closets behind the bathroom's walls offer possibilities for expanding the bathroom's size.*
Below: *By expanding into the closet of the left bedroom, there is enough room to include a generous vanity on one side of the room and add shelves to a corner.*

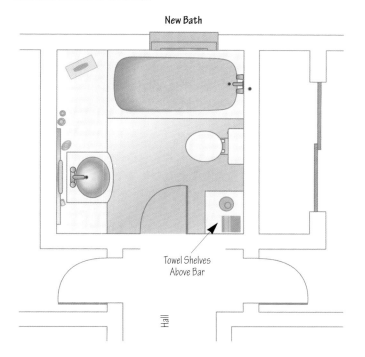

New Bath

Towel Shelves
Above Bar

cumbered floor space. However, it will be the costliest. One way to save money is to bump out the wall by a few feet and extend the existing floor structure out over the foundation. Consult an architect or builder, first, to make sure the structure is sound and can carry the additional load. Always inquire about local zoning ordinances that may affect your plans before proceeding. If you violate codes, you could be forced to remove the new construction.

CAN'T ADD-ON?

If you can't improve the layout of an existing bath by building an addition, take a good look at areas that are adjacent to the room, such as hallways or unused space under a stairway. Sometimes even a small amount of space stolen from a closet or an adjacent room can be the answer to your problem. If your family requires two bathrooms but there's only enough room for one, forego a spacious master bath for two smaller, side-by-side bathrooms. You'll save money this way, too, because the plumbing lines for both rooms will be right there.

REARRANGING AN EXISTING LAYOUT

If the existing floor plan works for you, all you have to think about is updating old fixtures, installing new tile, and perhaps replacing the cabinetry. Even so, you may want to play around with the idea of modifying the layout on paper. You may be surprised to discover, in fact, that a few minor changes in the floor plan can enhance your original arrangement. Just keep in mind: Moving plumbing fixtures in an existing bath may significantly raise costs.

SMART STEPS

ONE: *Make a new base drawing.* Like the base drawing you made for the old bathroom, use a ¹/₂-inch scale. If you are using a ¹/₄-inch grid, each square represents a 6-inch square of real floor space. Begin by drawing the outer walls, and then add the windows and doors.

TWO: *Make templates of the fixtures.* Paper templates of fixtures and cabinets are an easy way to experiment

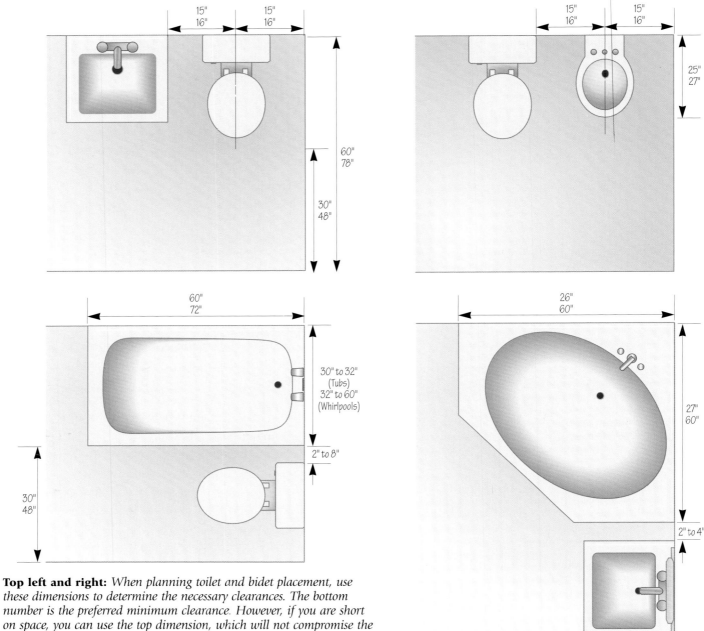

Top left and right: *When planning toilet and bidet placement, use these dimensions to determine the necessary clearances. The bottom number is the preferred minimum clearance. However, if you are short on space, you can use the top dimension, which will not compromise the accessibility of the layout for most people.*

Bottom left and right: *Use these clearances for rectangular tubs and whirlpools and corner tubs. Try to allow more space than the minimum clearance required by code—the smaller dimension.*

with different layouts. First draw the fixtures to scale on graph paper, and then cut them out so you can move them around your plan. If you have collected pictures and spec sheets (printed product information from the manufacturer), use the dimensions given. When cutting out templates,

include both the fixtures and the required front and side clearances—that way you won't get caught short. Usually, plumbing codes require a minimum clearance for each fixture. Fixture clearances are shown in the drawings on this and the next two pages. The top number of each pair indi-

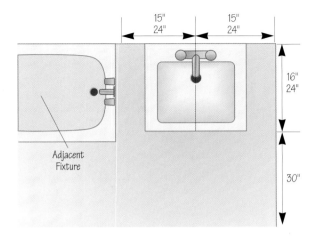

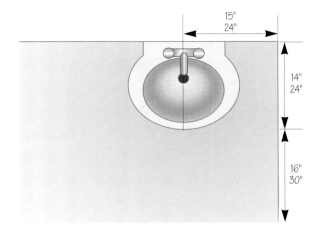

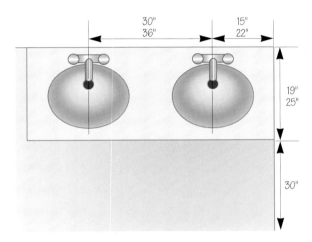

Clockwise from the top left: *If you don't have a specific lavatory in mind, use these general clearances for wall-hung, freestanding, and vanity-mounted units. The larger dimension is the preferred clearance, but if necessary, the smaller dimension can be used.*

length of the tub perpendicular to the joists to distribute the weight safely. If you don't, you'll incur the costs of adding structural support to the floor.) To make the tub the focal point of the room, put it opposite the door or within a direct line of view from the door. If there will be a separate tub and shower, locate them near each other so that they can share plumbing lines and the same sight lines. This also makes it easier to plan the space around them.

After placing the big items, locate your lavatory. Do you want two lavs or just one? Do you want two lavatories near each other or located on opposite sides of the room? Do you want two toilets? Will two people use the room at once? Answer these questions before you pencil in the location.

cates the minimum required by code or function. The bottom dimension allows more room between fixtures. For an efficient but convenient layout, aim for somewhere between the two numbers when you draw your plan, if the size of your bathroom permits.

THREE: *Place the fixtures.* You will use some fixtures more often than others: first the lavatory, next the toilet, then the tub or shower. An efficient plan places the lav closest to the door, followed by the toilet, and finally the tub, which is located the farthest away. If there is any leeway in your plan, place the toilet so that it will not be visible when the door is open. Even in a small bathroom, the direction of the door swing can help shield the toilet from view. Another easy way to place fixtures on your plan is to start with the largest ones. If you know you want a whirlpool bath and separate dual shower, pencil them in first. (Hint: Position the

Smart Tip About Planning

The easiest and least costly remodels take advantage of the existing water supplies, drain lines, and vent stacks. If you want to add a bath or expand one, try locating it next to an existing one. Even stacking the rooms one over the other on different floors can take advantage of the existing lines and lower the cost of building or rebuilding the bath. Another cost-cutting measure is limiting the plumbing fixtures to two walls. This avoids the need for —and expense of—additional plumbing lines.

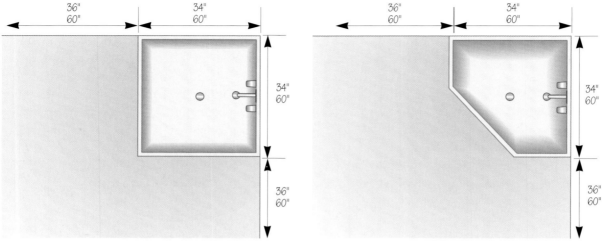

Left and far left:
Shower dimensions vary widely from the minimum usable size to the most generous. When space is tight, consider a corner unit. Don't forget to plan for clearance; the smaller dimension is the minimum clearance needed.

If you are placing two lavatories side by side, leave enough maneuvering space and elbow room. One smart way to do this is to install storage between them. Some families install two lavatories at different heights. Not only is this more comfortable and ergonomic, it defines space as adult-designated or child-designated in a bathroom shared by all.

Once you have the lavatories in place, go ahead and locate the toilet and bidet, if you have one. (A bidet resembles a toilet, but is actually a basinlike device for personal hygiene.) The bidet is another item you will want to keep away from the bathroom door and out of its sight line.

With the main elements penciled in, start adding the extras—the windows, doors, greenhouse, gym, sauna, and whatever other amenities you are considering. You can play with the design as long as you like, trying different ideas and placements, as long as you take practical matters like pipes and codes into consideration.

Although there are recommended guidelines for comfort and convenience, only you will be able to determine what will be most comfortable for you. If you happen to be 7 feet tall, you can probably forget about the height clearances and raise them! Likewise, if you are a small person, lower the counters. Don't worry about being able to resell your home later; another person of your height may appreciate the comfort of a higher or lower surface. If the need arises, installing a new vanity with standard-height countertop is not easy, but it's not a major project either.

Right: *This bathroom allows full view of the toilet from outside the room.*
Far right: *Better privacy is obtained by flopping the toilet and the sink and reversing the door swing.*

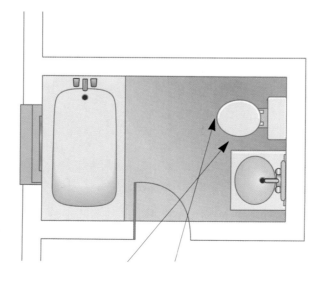

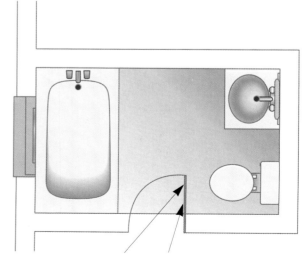

BASIC BATH ARRANGEMENTS

The most-common-size American bathroom measures 60x84 inches or 60x96 inches. The most common complaint about it is the lack of space. The arrangement may have suited families fifty years ago, but times and habits have changed. If it's the only bathroom in the house, making it work better becomes even more important.

When planning the layout, try angling a sink or shower unit in a corner to free up some floor space. Also, consider installing a pocket door. Instead of a traditional door that swings into the room and takes up wall space when it is open, a pocket door slides into the wall. Another smart way to add function to a small bathroom is to install a pocket door into a wall between the toilet and the sink. That way two people can use the room at the same time.

You can also make a small bathroom feel roomier by bringing in natural light with a skylight or roof window or by replacing one small standard window with several small casement units that can be installed high on the wall to maintain privacy.

If you are adding a second or possibly a third bathroom to your house, here are a few other ideas for your consideration— and inspiration.

Right: *When a powder room is located right off the public areas of the house, sight lines from the door are important.*

THE POWDER ROOM

The guest bath. The half bath. It has a lot of names, and it may be the most efficient room in the house, providing just what you need often in tight quarters. A powder room normally includes nothing more than a lavatory and a toilet. You can find small-scale fixtures specifically designed for it, from the tiniest lavs to unusually narrow toilets. In general,

however, maintain a clearance that meets code on each side of the toilet and include comfortable reaching room for the toilet-paper dispenser. Most powder rooms measure at least 36 inches wide by 54 to 60 inches long, depending on the layout of the space.

Keep a small powder room as light and open as possible. Make sure the door swings out against a wall, or use a pocket door for easy access. If it must be accessible for someone in a wheelchair, include a minimum 5-foot-diameter circle of space in the center of the room, which is just large enough for turning around.

Because the powder room is often for guests and is normally located on the ground floor near the living area, take extra care to ensure privacy. The best location is in a hallway away from the living room, kitchen, and dining area.

A CHILDREN'S BATH

What should be included in a children's bath plan depends on the ages and number of children using it. If the bath will be for only one child, the design is easy. You can tailor it to him or her, taking care to plan for growing and changing needs. Anticipate the storage and lighting requirements of an older child's self-grooming habits, for example. However, if more than one child will use this bathroom, consider their genders, and whether more than two will be using the bath at the same time. How many lavatories do you really need? The answer is at least two, if not more. The best designs for growing children include compartmentalized spaces—one for the toilet, one for the bath, and one for the lavatories. If this isn't feasible given the existing space, at least try to set the toilet apart. That way the children can take turns going to the bathroom and brushing their teeth for speedier bedtimes.

Right: *A little girl's favorite things inspired the decorations of her bathroom.*
Opposite: *The same designer incorporated a nautical theme into a bath shared by two boys.*

Two special considerations in a kid's bath are territorial issues and safety. Children are famous for protecting their space. Rather than fight this natural tendency, plan a cabinet drawer or wall shelf for each child. For safety, you may want to install countertops and sinks lower than standard height or build a step into the vanity cabinet's toekick area. Review other recommendations set forth in Chapter Three, "Safety and Universal Design." Lastly, remember what it was like to be a child. Get down to a kid's level and design for a youngster's height and capabilities. Consult your children about decisions regarding the room's decoration. Ask their opinions on color and wallpaper patterns, for example.

THE FAMILY BATH

Compartmentalizing is the best way to start planning the family bath. But remember, when you separate the bathroom into smaller, distinct areas, you run the risk of making the room feel cramped. Try to alleviate this with extra natural light, good artificial lighting, and translucent partitions made of glass blocks or etched glass. Anything that divides with privacy while also allowing light to enter will help ease the closed-in feeling.

If separating the fixtures is not possible, include a sink in the dressing area within the master bedroom to provide a second place for applying makeup or shaving. Investigate building a back-to-back bath in lieu of one large shared room. Another popular option is to locate the bathing fix-

Above and right: *This family bath makes the most of its floor space. A double vanity and lots of storage offers room for two. On the other side of the room, the shower is located across from the toilet, which has a half wall for privacy (insets).*
Opposite: *Convenience and charm go hand in hand in this nostalgic family bathroom. The telephone-style faucet and sprayer in the tub is great for washing the kids' hair or even for bathing the family mutt.*

tures, both the tub and separate shower, in the center of the room; install the bidet, a toilet, and sink on either side in their own separate areas. To make the arrangement work, keep each side of the room accessible to the door.

THE MASTER BATH

The concept of the master bath has come of age in the past decade. It is one of the most popular rooms to remodel, and gives one of the highest returns on investment upon resale. It's where you can create that sought-after getaway—the home version of a European spa.

Some popular amenities to include in your plan are a sauna, greenhouse, exercise studio, fireplace, audio and video systems, faucets and sprayers with full massaging options, steam room, whirlpool tub, and dressing table. You are only limited by size and imagination—and some local codes.

Extras can be tempting but may require special planning. For example, you may need additional support in the floor, as well as supplemental heating and ventilation. You wouldn't want to slip into a tub and have it fall two floors to the middle of the living room. Unfortunately, this really does happen when the weight of an oversized contemporary tub is installed on top of a fifty-year-old floor. Older houses simply weren't built to accommodate the volume of water some people now use when bathing.

Some of the best floor plans for the modern adult bath also include a separate room for the toilet and bidet, a detached tub and shower, and dual sinks on opposite sides of the room with adjacent dressing rooms and walk-in closets. Modern couples want to share a master bed and bath, but they also want to have privacy and the ease of getting ready in the morning without tripping over their mates. The only way to do this harmoniously is to mingle the parts of the room that invite sharing and separate those elements that are always private.

Opposite, bottom: *Include natural light whenever possible. Small casements high on the wall won't compromise privacy in a bathing area.*
Opposite, top: *A large Palladian-style window over the sink makes a beautiful architectural statement.*
Right and inset: *The same bath refrains from a closed-in look by using a glass shower and interior transom-style window over the tub.*

SAFETY &
UNIVERSAL
DESIGN

Wet floors. Bare feet. Various stages of dress. Contact lenses in, contact lenses out. Sleepy nights, groggy mornings. Electrical appliances in close proximity to water. These are some of the reasons why more accidents occur in the bathroom than in any other room in the house. They are also safety concerns to be considered when designing a new bath. This is especially true when those who will be using it are the most vulnerable: children and the elderly. Slips, falls, and hot-water scalds top the injury list.

Universal design addresses the needs of multigenerational households. As Baby Boomers bring their aging parents home to live while still raising families of their own, it is not uncommon to have small children and grandparents living under the same roof at the same time. Indeed, as our population ages, in general, it behooves everyone to think about design that is usable by each member of the family, today and in the future.

SAFETY FIRST

While form and function are always the two critical parts of any design, safety should reign as a primary factor in any bathroom remodel. Minimizing the risk of bodily injury only makes good sense. It's the smart choice. Take the following steps when designing for safety. And remember, you don't have to be very young or very old to be at risk of accidents, particularly in the bathroom.

SMART STEPS

ONE: *Use slip-resistant flooring material.* Slips and falls are two of the top three on the injury hit list, so a good flooring choice is critical. Choose a slip-resistant surface such as textured tile or vinyl, or a matte-finish laminate flooring. If you decide on ceramic tile, be sure to purchase the type designed for flooring. Place bath mats and rugs with non-skid backings throughout the room.

TWO: *Install grab bars.* With the aging of society, grab bars are becoming standard accessories in bathrooms. If you don't need them now, you may in the future—even if it is only while you are recuperating from a sports injury or during the last few months of a pregnancy. Consider

installing grab bars inside each tub and shower. You may even think about locating grab bars in the toilet area, particularly if there are people in your household who may have difficulty getting up and down.

Many manufacturers offer grab bars in a variety of decorative styles and finishes. The good news is that they can also double as towel racks for added storage. But make sure walls are reinforced to receive the added stress of a person's

Previous page: *A childs' bath can be cheerful and safe.*
Below: *A pressure-balanced shower control equalizes hot and cold water levels.*
Left: *Antiscalding devices (shown stacked on the edge of a tub) keep water comfortably temperate.*
Opposite: *In a master bath, a grab bar that coordinates handsomely with other fittings assists in getting in and out of the tub.*

efore installing grab bars. *Never use towel racks as substitutes for grab bars.*

THREE: *Regulate water temperature—and devices.* Regulating scalding temperatures in a tub or sink faucet is essential in any home, but especially

when there are children or elderly persons using the bath. Install faucets with antiscald devices that prevent water temperatures from rising over 111 degrees Fahrenheit, or opt for pressure-balanced valves that equalize hot and cold water. Consider a faucet that can be preprogrammed by you to a specific temperature. These controls should be childproof.

Besides opting for a faucet with a temperature regulator, you can prevent other related mishaps by installing tub and shower controls so they are accessible from inside and outside the fixtures. The NKBA recommends locating shower controls between 38 and 48 inches above the floor and offset toward the room. For tub controls, place them between the tub rim and 33 inches above the floor, below the grab bar. Like shower controls, they should be installed offset toward

Left: *Plan to enjoy your new shower safely. A permanent bench in this one is within reach of shampoo in the built-in nook.*
Above: *A stylish alternative, this rust-proof chair must have rubber pads under the feet to keep it stationary. An adjustable-height shower that converts to a hand-held sprayer allows someone seated to rinse off without bending.*
Right: *Although equipped with a ground-fault circuit interrupter, this bathroom's electrical plug is dangerously close to the sink.*

the room. That way someone outside the tub or shower—or in a wheelchair—can regulate the controls as necessary.

FOUR: *Choose shatter-resistant materials.* Select tempered or laminated glass, plastic, or other shatterproof materials. Try to avoid any material or product that may break and present another hazard on top of a fall. This is particularly true in children's baths. Children tend to get rambunctious and exert more wear and tear on materials than a manufacturer may have anticipated. (Always choose durable, impact-resistant materials and fixtures in any child's room.) If you can, opt for a child-safe product over a luxury item if you can't afford both.

FIVE: *Design a safe shower environment.* Besides shatterproof doors that open into the room, not into the shower, and temperature-control devices, there are other measures you can take to make showering pleasant and safe. For example, every shower unit should have a seat or bench that is 17 inches to 19 inches high and 15 inches deep, according to the NKBA. That way you won't put yourself at risk by standing on a soapy, slippery surface. Your back will thank you, too, when you don't strain it with deep bending at the waist to reach your feet.

Of course, you'll want a shower that is equipped with the latest in jetted sprayers and shower heads to look glamorous as it functions, but keep the design simple. Avoid steps, install safety rails, and make the entrance wide enough to get in and out comfortably. Specify a 60-inch-wide entrance for a shower that measures 36 inches deep. For a compact 32-inch-deep shower, plan an entrance that is 42 inches wide.

SIX: *Plan a safe tub.* It's not hard to feel like Cleopatra soaking in a luxurious sunk-in tub. And certainly a tub set into a sumptuous platform makes a big fashion statement. But the reality is that a tub that requires you to step up or down stairs can be hazardous, if steps are wet and slippery or if your body is off balance. When children will be bathing, supervision is a must. You may want to reconsider this design, especially if you will remain in the house as you age. What appears glamorous now could be impractical and dangerous when you're older.

SEVEN: *Keep electrical switches, plugs, and lighting fixtures away from water sources and wet hands.* Not only that, but make sure every electrical receptacle is grounded and protected with ground-fault circuit interrupters. These devices can cut the electrical current if there is a power surge or if moisture is present. Most building codes require installing them in kitchens, bathrooms, and any other rooms with plumbing to protect homeowners against the danger of electrical shock.

Planning to include a light fixture above the tub or in the shower? For safety's sake, install it so that it is not within the reach of anyone—in either a sitting or standing position. Check local codes regarding this option.

EIGHT: *Don't clutter the traffic area.* Be realistic, no matter how clever you are about using every square inch of space. If your bathroom is a compact 40 square feet, it can't accommodate an oversize tub or a bidet. Don't crowd in extra amenities and risk tripping over yourself or clogging walkways in the bathroom. There are minimum clearances you should adhere to for your own safety. (See "Creating Functional Space," in Chapter Three.) An adjacent toilet/bidet installation, for example, requires a 16 inch minimum clearance to all obstructions. A water closet (toilet compartment) should be at least 3 feet wide by 15½ feet long with a swing-out door.

NINE: *Make storage accessible.* If you can't reach a storage area without standing on the toilet, it's not useful. Ideally, storage for toiletries, linens, and the like should be no higher than 4 feet from the floor. Don't make it too low, either. You can avoid ill-advised bending by keeping storage at least 15 inches from the floor, says the NKBA.

Locate storage for personal hygiene products within the reach of a person who is seated on a bidet or a toilet.

TEN: *Install a safety lock on the door.* For some reason the words, "Do not lock the door," trigger an irresistible urge in children to do just the opposite. The best solution is to install a safety lock. This device, which is inexpensive, looks just like a standard door knob with a little push-button lock on the inside of the bathroom and a pin hole in the knob on the outside. To release the lock from outside the door, all you have to do is insert the tip of a thin screwdriver or any other object that will fit into the hole, and push out the button.

Lastly, use common sense. Some things should be obvious but are often overlooked. For example, people come in all sizes. Take an inventory of family members' heights to avoid placing sharp corners or racks at eye level. Children tend to grow, however, so this presents a challenge. The best approach is to

Left: *An accessible bath can be glamorous, too. For wheelchair accessibility at the vanity, the design adheres to a minimum knee width that is 30 inches wide.*
Opposite: *The full-length, mirrored-door cabinet features theatrical lights around the frame and opens to accessible storage.*

place sharp-cornered items in spots that are away from any traffic patterns. For example, don't put a counter next to the tub where you will bump your hip every day as you step out of the shower.

Designing for safety is not difficult. All you need is a little thought and foresight. Run through the list of your family's functional needs for the bath, and then consider your physical safety. Is there a better way to arrange fixtures that will make it easier to maneuver? Does the design you have sketched out contain enough space for two people to use the bathroom at the same time? Answer these questions now, not after the fixtures have been installed.

UNIVERSAL DESIGN

By the year 2006, fully one-third of America will be either disabled, chronically ill, or over the age of 65. Our society is aging, and our current housing stock is not designed to meet their changing capabilities. That is why the smartest trend in remodeling these days is universal design—an approach that opens the bath, indeed the entire home, to people of all different capabilities.

Universal-designed bathrooms are not the same as "accessible" ones. (See next page.) They are simply more accommodating to people of all ages, sizes, skills, and capabilities. Begin by analyzing your lifestyle and your family's unique needs. Do you have someone in your house who must sit down while putting on makeup or shaving? Plan kneespace under a sink or vanity. Does anyone have balance problems stepping into a tub? Install safety rails. Do you have small children who want to get ready for bed all by themselves without help from Mom? Perhaps a lower countertop and sink would encourage independence. Are you planning on having children in the future? What features would make your home more comfortable during pregnancy and your baby's infancy? Will you really be able to step

into a sunk-in tub for a hand-held shower during your ninth month? Maybe a separate tub and shower are more practical for the times you will be pregnant.

Before incorporating every universal design idea you can think of into your bath, decide how long you want to remain in the house. Statistics show that more often than not, today's homeowners stay put longer. If you plan on keeping your house into your golden years, include some accessible features. Good ideas include digital displays, which are easier to read; wider doorways to accommodate walkers, crutches, and wheelchairs; and minimum thresholds on interior and exterior doorways for easy maneuvering. The items specified in a universal design are usable by most people regardless of their level of ability or disability. For example, everyone can use lever door handles more easily than round ones, from people who have no hands to those whose hands are full. Universal design refers to products or to a more conve-

Opposite: *A padded seat can be used during all or part of a shower.*
Left: *In this accessible bathroom, there is enough clear floor space to allow transfer from a wheelchair onto the toilet, using grab bars for support.*

budget, don't add them. But remember safety—and keep the grab bars for days when you aren't so steady on your feet.

You may have heard the terms "accessible" and "adaptable" bandied about as though they are interchangeable with each other and with "universal design." In fact, they are different.

ACCESSIBLE DESIGN
Accessible design normally means that a home—or in this case a bathroom—is barrier-free. It also indicates that the room complies with the design guidelines for disabled people found in government regulations, such as the American National Standards Institute's A117.1 (ANSI A117.1-1986). There are a number of guidelines governing accessible design. Their goal is to provide criteria for designing for people who must use wheelchairs. Most accessible homes incorporate a number of fixed features that enable a disabled person easy access.

If there is a disabled person in your family who will be using the new bathroom, you'll have to plan space accordingly, making sure there is adequate room for them to move around. You'll also need fixtures and fittings that allow people to care for themselves independently.

In addition to the safety features recommended earlier in this chapter, there are specific accessible-design guidelines, recommended by the NKBA, that you should follow. Begin by including enough space in your floor plan for a wheelchair-bound person to enter and maneuver around. Start with the entry. Doorways must be a minimum of 32 inches wide. Once inside, the person will need a passage that is

nient placement of fixtures. Changing the counter heights in a bath may be more ergonomic for a couple whose heights are drastically different. The same would be true about placing a shower head. Universal design addresses the scope of accessibility and attempts to make all elements and spaces usable by all people.

It may be worthwhile to look into some of the smart home technology—new products that allow you to call your home from your cellular phone to turn on the lights, raise the thermostat, start running a bath, preprogram water level and temperature, and turn on the oven for dinner so you have time for that long, hot soak. There are thousands of ways to make a home more usable. The key is to look at universal-designed products and match them to your house, your capabilities, and your anticipated future needs. Whatever you do, remember that universal design is supposed to make life easier. If adding these features will destroy your

Below: *A high arc faucet permits someone to wash his or her hair comfortably at the sink. Wrist-blade faucet handles are easier to use than those that require turning with a hand.*

at least 24 inches deep, moving into the room, and 36 inches wide. When you are sketching out the plan, include enough space for someone in a wheelchair to open or close the door. Because the amount of space depends on the type of door and the approach into the bathroom, you'll have to work it out with the disabled person in your

home. Perhaps there is a similar entry into another room in the house where he or she can practice entering, closing, and opening the door while you take the measurements of the door swing.

With regard to fixture placement, the recommendations for clear floor space offered by the NKBA are listed in the box on this page. Just remember two things: First, it's okay to overlap clearances for different fixtures. Second, although you should always try to adhere to these professional guidelines, the available space may limit you. If you have to deviate a few inches here or there, the bathroom will still be the most accessible you can make it. When you are ready to shop for fixtures and fittings, keep in mind you get what you pay for. As with products for standard bathrooms, there is an array (though more limited) that range from the purely practical to technological marvels.

In general, shop for a tub that allows a disabled person to transfer from a wheelchair to the bath with ease. There are tubs constructed with built-in seats that lift and rotate, allowing a person to slide on, rotate into the unit, and lower himself hydraulically flush with the bottom of the tub. This position is the most comfortable for bathing. A hand-held sprayer will be handy, too, for warming up the water or rinsing hair.

Transfer showers permit a wheelchair-bound person to roll next to the unit, adjust the controls from the outside, and then back up and make a parallel transfer onto the shower seat using grab bars—or the wheelchair—as support. Standing individuals can use the shower by flipping down the seat.

In the toilet area, you'll have choices, too. Instead of the standard 15-inch-high toilet, choose an 18-inch-high model which makes getting up and down easier—even for people who are not disabled. Add a flush-handle extension and install a toilet-paper holder with a controlled-flow feature. For accessibility, locate it 26 inches high on a wall in front of the toilet. A wall-mounted sink, or one dropped into a countertop, should be replaced at the universal-access height—32 inches. To accommodate someone in a wheelchair, plan a minimum 27-inch-deep by

30-inches-wide minimum knee space under the vanity or sink. Insulate any exposed undersink pipes to prevent burning. Lever faucets or touch-pad controls are recommended. If your budget permits, install touchless electronic faucets that sense motion. It's also practical to include a sprayer so that hair can be washed at the lav.

ADAPTABLE DESIGN

Adaptable designs are those that can be easily modified for use by a disabled person. They are normally used in multifamily rental housing so the landlord can rent to a nondisabled person as well as a disabled one. The adaptable house incorporates some concealment of traditional accessible features. For example, an adaptable bath would have a door on the vanity underneath the sink that could be removed to make room for a wheelchair. There may be no steps at the tub and shower area—a good idea in every situation—or doorways may be extra wide.

Accessible Fixture Placement

The table below shows the minimum floor clearances, in inches, recommended by the National Kitchen and Bath Association for placing fixtures in an accessible bathroom. Use them as guidelines, but tailor them to your personal situation, available space, and needs as necessary.

Fixture	NKBA Minimum
Lavatory	30x48*
Toilet	48x48**
Bidet	48x48***
Bathtub	60x30****
Shower	

In the case of a shower that is less than 60 inches wide, the minimum clearance should be 36 inches deep by the width of the shower plus 12 inches. A shower that is more than 60 inches wide requires 36 inches of clear floor space by the width of the shower.

*Up to 19 inches can extend under the lavatory.

**At least 16 inches must extend to each centerline of the toilet.

***You may reduce it to 30x48 if space is tight, but that may compromise full use.

****For a parallel approach. For a perpendicular approach, clearance should be 60x48.

LIGHT BY DESIGN

Bathrooms are perfect places to play with light and its effects. There are so many elements that can capture light, reflect it, and refract it. Unfortunately, many homeowners overlook the importance of lighting design in the bathroom. Like any other room in the house, the bath deserves a deliberate, studied plan. Good bathroom lighting brightens the space, makes it safe, and creates a pleas-ant, comfortable atmosphere. With the bathroom evolving into a larger, more elegant space over the past decade, it now calls for decorative lighting, as well.

In this chapter, we'll explore the types of lighting and how you can use each one effectively to create a functional and unique lighting plan for your new bathroom.

NATURAL LIGHT

The most natural light source and the best complement to your bathroom is daylight. Everybody loves a sunny, cheerful room. Not only does it look better, but it makes you feel better. Imagine drenching yourself in light as you take your morning shower. Thankfully, modern technology has greatly enhanced glazing options with low-E glass to solve the problem of drafty, inefficient windows. Today it is possible to capture the daylight, as well as beautiful views, and incorporate them into your design without worrying about losing heat or air conditioning.

If privacy allows, a large window, a bay, or a bank of smaller units adjacent to the tub adds to the luxuriousness of the room. In a contemporary setting, install clean-lined casement windows. To blend with a traditional decor, consider an elegant arched window or a standard

Previous page: *A multilayered lighting design, incorporating many lamps and fixtures, personalizes a large plan.*
Left: *An arched window opens up a bumped-out bathing area to a lush, private garden outside.*
Opposite: *In a large space, multiple recessed ceiling fixtures are required for adequate general illumination.*

double-hung unit with muntins. If your bathroom will be adjacent to a patio, deck, a hot tub, or private garden, think about including a pair of French or sliding doors in your plans.

Take a good look at the view you will be bringing indoors by adding or enlarging a window. Of course, not every house overlooks the ocean or snow-capped mountains, but even a pretty tree in the backyard and a few well positioned plants can make the view more pleasing. However, if your house is too close to the neighbors, a skylight, roof window, or glass blocks may be a better way to introduce natural light into the bath without compromising privacy or aesthetics.

No matter how much natural light you may have in the bathroom, there are times when you'll have to supplement it with artificial lighting. In fact, artificial lighting actually can enhance the effect of natural light at times.

THE MAIN TYPES OF ARTIFICIAL LIGHT

Lighting is the easiest way to set or change a mood. With one switch, your bathroom can go from a bright and busy grooming center to a softly lit, calm, and quiet getaway.

If you've incorporated a variety of lighting options in other areas of the house but have neglected to do the same in your existing bathroom, now is a perfect opportunity. But first, you must understand the options created by the four main types of artificial light.

❦ Ambient lighting. Ambient, or general, lighting is illumination that fills an entire room. The source is normally from an overhead fixture, but the light itself does not appear

to come from any one particular direction. Ambient light surrounds a room generally, not specifically. The most obvious example is fluorescent strips in the average office environment. A covering over the strips hides the source and diffuses the light throughout the room.

A wall sconce is another good example of ambient light. The fixture washes light up the wall for an overall glow. The wall reflects the light, which diminishes the appear-

ance of a single source. While you can tell light is coming from the sconce, the overall glow produced is diffused or softened.

The key to good ambient lighting is making it inconspicuous. It is merely the backdrop for the rest of the room, not the main feature. It changes with the surrounding environment— always providing light, but never becoming obvious. For example, ambient lighting used during the day should blend in with the amount of natural light entering the room. At night, you should be able to adjust the light level inside the home so it doesn't contrast jarringly with the darkness outside.

❧ Task lighting. As the name implies, task lighting is purely functional in purpose. It illuminates a specific area for a particular job, such as putting in contact lenses, reading in the tub, shaving, or applying makeup.

Theatrical lighting around vanity mirrors is an excellent example of task lighting. It provides

Left: *A strip of decorative miniature lights in the toekick area under a vanity artfully contrasts with the dramatic, dark surfaces.*
Above and right: *Wall sconces installed in the vanity areas cast the kind of soft, diffused glow that enhances skin tones.*

cross illumination, while avoiding the distorting shadows that overhead lighting often produces.

Task lighting should always be included in a lighting plan for the bath, but its use should be optional. In other words, you can turn it on when you need it, and keep it off at other times. That's why task lights should not be on

Below: *Small lights mounted under the tub reflect onto the floor and create a focal point at the bath.*
Opposite: *Fiber optics in the ceiling cove resemble twinkling stars in the heavens, while mini spotlights recessed into the soffits wash the walls with "moonlight."*

the same switch with a fixture that provides general illumination. The effect of having both on at once is bright and too harsh. It's not the kind of lighting environment that is conducive to grooming routines. To make it easy to see what you're doing, an individual fixture has to concentrate the light toward a limited—not general—area.

❧ Accent lighting. Often the most forgotten in the bath, but always the most dramatic, accent lighting draws attention to a particular element in the room, such as a handsome architectural feature or a work of art. You may ask, Why would I want to do that? The answer is atmosphere. Accent lighting makes a room come alive. It creates a mood. It shapes space. For example, small uplights placed inconspicuously under a potted plant create an

artful interplay of light and shadows on the wall and ceiling. Lights recessed into a soffit above a vanity cast a downward glow of illumination over a gorgeous countertop without spilling light into the rest of the room. Cove lighting installed above a tub shimmers over the water and delineates a bathing area dramatically.

Without accent lighting, there may be light but no focus, no character, no show business. With it, a design becomes exciting, theatrical, and rich.

Left: *Lamps installed over a tub provide good lighting for reading while you're taking a long, hot soak. Make sure they comply with local codes if you plan to install them.*
Above: *Vertical strips of theatrical lights are perfect for grooming tasks, especially when on both sides of a vanity mirror.*
Opposite: *A small spotlight inside a recessed area makes even a simple vase and a few flowers look artful. Lights installed underneath the contemporary glass countertop create a big design impact.*

☙ Decorative lighting. Where accent lighting draws attention to another object or surface, decorative lighting draws attention to itself. It can be kinetic, in the form of candles or a fireplace, or static, such as a fixed wall candelabra. Because it commands notice, it can attract or distract attention to or from something else. In this sense, it can be functional.

You can use decorative lighting in the bath to draw the eye upward toward a cathedral ceiling or to distract attention from the toilet and bidet, for example. By capturing your eye, decorative lighting forces your focus away from everything else. It doesn't highlight the way accent lighting does, and it doesn't provide a great deal of illumination as does ambient lighting. Decorative lighting is the device most lighting designers love to use—the final stroke in a multilayered plan that combines more than one kind of lighting.

Some examples of decorative lighting include candles, chandeliers, neon sculptures or signs, a strip of miniature lights—any type of light that is deliberate and contrived. Include it to unify a room—to strike a balance among all the types of lighting in the room, including natural light from the sun and moon.

THE ROLE OF BULBS IN DESIGN

Just changing the types of bulbs, or lamps as professional lighting designers call them, in your existing bathroom fixtures can make a major difference in the way the room looks, functions, and feels. Does this mean you should go out and replace all of your fluorescent lamps with halogen fixtures and call off the rest of your remodeling plans? That might be exaggerating the power of the right lighting design. But don't underestimate it, either.

Understanding the differences in lamps will help you select the right light sources for every area in your bath. Light is like paint. You get different effects depending on the combinations of bulbs and fixtures you use. And color is nothing but the reflection of different types of light.

When selecting bulbs for a lighting scheme for your bath, always consider the important relationship that exists between color and light.

matched. You will also be able to vary the coolness or warmth of lighting for specific situations. Generally, light sources that are rated below 3,000K are considered warm, while those with ratings above 4,100K are perceived as cool. The recommended range for light sources falls between 3,000 and 3,500K.

STANDARD MEASUREMENTS FOR COLOR

Scales used universally in lighting assess the color temperature the lamp gives off and how light from the lamp affects the objects it is lighting. The term "Correlated Color Temperature" (CCT) is used to compare the color appearance of light in terms of warmth or coolness. Lamps, which range in color from red to orange to yellow to blue to blue-white, are designated according to the Kelvin (K) temperature scale. This will help you to select lamps that are closely

Above: *Deluxe warm white fluorescent strips on either side of a mirror cast a more natural glow than conventional fluorescent bulbs, which appear almost blue.*
Right: *In a master bath, multiple overheads and vertical strips in strategic places over the vanities are effective for general and task lighting.*

Color rendition describes how a light source affects the perception of the color of an object it illuminates. The Color Rendition Index (CRI) is a way of measuring a lamp's ability to render true color (the color of an object in sunlight). The color-rendering capabilities of lamps are rated from 1 to 100. True color is 100.

TYPES OF BULBS

Most homes include a combination of warm and cool tones, so selecting bulbs that provide balanced lighting comfortably close to what appears normal to the eye is usually the most attractive choice. Experiment with various combinations of bulbs to create your own desired effect. This kind of layering and balance are two keys to a successful and sophisticated lighting plan for your bath. Here's a description of the most common types of bulbs and their characteristics, advantages, and disadvantages.

❧ Incandescent. Like sunlight, incandescent bulbs emit "continuous-spectrum light," or light that contains every color. Illumination from these bulbs, in fact, is even warmer than sunlight, making its effect very appealing in a room. It makes our skin tones look good and even enhances our feeling of well-being. The drawbacks to incandescent bulbs are that they use a lot of electricity and produce a lot of heat. However, they come in a variety of shapes, sizes, and applications. (One type features a waterproof lens cover that makes it suitable for over a tub or inside a shower.) These bulbs can be clear, diffuse, tinted, or colored, and they may have a reflective coating inside.

❧ Fluorescent. These energy-efficient bulbs cast a diffuse, shadowless light that makes them great for general illumination. They are very eeconomical, but the old standard fluorescents are quite unflattering, making everything and everyone appear bluish and bland. There are newer fluorescent bulbs, called deluxe warm white or warm white, that are warmer and more natural in rendering color that more closely resembles true sunlight. Mixing these bulbs with incandescent lamps, plus adding as much natural light to the plan as possible, can make them much more appealing.

Above: *The up-and-down light cast by fixtures on two opposite walls perpendicular to the mirror create pleasant indirect lighting that is reflected off the pale surfaces of the walls, countertop, and wood cabinetry.*
Right: *Candelabra-style wall sconces enhance the romantic appeal of this bath, casting a soft, candlelike glow.*

In some parts of the country, local codes require fluorescent lights to conform to energy conservation mandates.

❦ Halogen. This is actually a type of incandescent lamp that operates at greater energy efficiency. It produces brighter, whiter light at a lower wattage. One disadvantage is a higher price tag. However, although halogens cost more up front, they last longer than conventional incandescents. Because a halogen bulb produces a higher heat output than other incandescents, it requires a special shielding. The low-voltage version of halogen bulbs produces a 50 percent brighter light than standard halogen bulbs. These are compact and use less electricity, which makes them more energy efficient, too. Low-voltage halogens are typically used for creative accent lighting in a room.

❦ Fiber optics. One of countless innovations gradually finding its way into the home, a fiber-optic system consists of one extremely bright lamp to transport light to one or more destinations through fiber-optic conduits. Used for accent lighting, fiber-optic lighting has the advantage of not generating excessive heat.

ASSESSING YOUR LIGHTING NEEDS

When a room is not bright enough, most people typically exchange low-watt light bulbs for high-watt versions. In a bathroom, with so many reflective surfaces, that may just create more glare. Wattage, in fact, is simply a measurement of how much electricity a lamp consumes. The light output of a bulb is measured in *lumens.* So why do people always talk in terms of watts? Because the higher the wattage, the greater the lumens. When looking for the intensity produced by a lamp refer to it's candlepower (Cp). The more candela (units), the brighter the source.

There are several important factors that will affect how much supplemental light you need. First, assess the reflectance levels in the room, or the amount of light that is reflected from a colored surface, such as tiles or a painted wall. Light colors are reflective, dark colors are absorbent. For example, white reflects 80 percent of the light in a room, while black reflects only 4 percent of it. In practical terms, a bathroom with a white vanity and tile and pale walls requires less light than one with dark cabinetry and tiles and dark walls.

Next, consider the size of the room. How high are the ceilings? High ceilings require brighter lights to dispel shadows. But you'll have to tone down the level of brightness in a room with low ceilings because light tends to bounce off low ceilings and walls. How many windows and skylights are there? Do they face the sunny south, or is their exposure to the north or somewhere in between?

There are no perfect stock formulas. But by looking at how each of these factors affects the others, you can make educated choices when developing your light plan. Keeping in mind the science and technology involved in lighting will help you assess your own requirements for the new bathroom. Ideally, you'll want to incorporate a variety of options for different activities, to create ambiance, and for decoration. Use the following steps to get started.

SMART STEPS

ONE: *Examine your activities.* Above all, your lighting design should enhance the function of the new bathroom. Try taking out a splinter or bandaging a cut without the right light. Make a list of your daily routines in the bathroom, from morning to night. If you will have a laundry hamper in the bathroom, will you sort clothes there? Do you need specific light for reading there?

TWO: *Sketch an informal plan.* Refer to the base map you drew of the bathroom or make a new sketch. (See Chapter Two, "Function: Up Close and Personal.") Circle the activity centers—the bath area, the sink, the dressing area, laundry center, and so forth. Everything you expect to do

will require a different level of light. For example, do you need strong light to differentiate between blue and black socks? Of course, you'll want to light the tub area to make it bright enough for stepping in and out safely, but would you prefer a softer glow while you relax? Something as simple as a dimmer switch may be all that's required.

Note each activity center with a G for general or ambient light, T for task light, A for accent light, and D for decorative light. In some places around the room, you may want to indicate more than one type of light.

Place your general lighting first, and then indicate where you'll need task lights. Start around the mirror. Plan lighting around the sides of the mirror for cross-illumination. This avoids the shadows that typically result from downlighting. Another tip: Never focus a light to shine directly in the mirror or on a highly polished chrome faucet. The reflection of the bouncing light will distract your attention.

After you've noted every activity center for task lighting, decide where to install accent lighting. You might want some recessed fixtures over the tub. Maybe you can highlight beautiful crown molding or hand-painted tile. If you want to use accent lighting but don't know where it should go, ask yourself what is the most interesting feature in your bathroom. It may be something as simple as a framed print on the wall, a collection of pretty perfume bottles on the vanity, or a display on a small shelf. This is strictly your call.

You don't have to place decorative lighting into your plan unless it is a wired fixture, such as a neon sculpture or a track system of low-voltage halogens. But if you know you'll be using candles in the bathroom, it is a good idea to indicate them, too. That way you can specify an appropriate niche that will hold them safely where they can't tip over.

Designers typically determine light needs by using suggested foot-candle (Fc) levels for different activities and areas. Foot-candles, which refer to the amount of light that falls on a surface, are used primarily for directional lamps. To determine the foot-candle power you need to light an area, divide the candlepower of the bulb by the distance from the fixture to surface squared ($Fc=Cp\div D^2$).

Above: *The color of lamp shades will affect the quality of light. Light-absorbing black shades on the fixtures keeps the room dim.* **Opposite:** *Conversely, gold-tone shades are more light reflective and create a brighter effect, which bounces more light around this vanity area.*

THREE: *Check your local code.* Every municipality has its own codes regarding the placement of light and electricity around water. Before you purchase any light fixtures, check with the building inspector for the local code or speak with your contractor, who should be familiar with these issues. If you violate code, you won't pass inspection.

FOUR: *Visit lighting showrooms.* The best way to get ideas is to visit lighting showrooms and the lighting department in home centers. This will give you a chance to take an inventory of fixture types and styles currently on the market. Also, you can take advantage of the advice of lighting specialists employed at these stores. They can help you create the right plan and style of lighting for your bathroom. Bring along your sketch, your list of activities, as well as the design notebook you have compiled containing clippings, notes, sample plans, color charts, tile, paint, and fabric samples. The lighting designer can assess what you're after from there.

As you might already expect, some in-store advice is free. Ask about it. A few suggestions may be all you need to steer you in the right direction. Otherwise, you may want to consider an in-home consultation. Inquire about fees, which may be surprisingly affordable. Sometimes a modest investment in professional advice pays off handsomely in the final result—and in the discount lighting designers can offer on the fixtures they sell.

There are also systems that computerize a variety of lighting options. A lighting specialist can design an entire program that sets the lights throughout the bathroom on a system devised for different moods and activities, such as showering, relaxing, exercising, washing the dog, or styling your hair. Everything is preprogrammed and controlled by one central panel. All you have to do is press the button corresponding to your selection. It definitely takes the guesswork out of layering light on your own. However, because of the sophisticated technology involved, these so-called "smart systems" can be high-priced, perhaps adding thousands of dollars to your budget.

FINDING THE RIGHT FIXTURE

Don't worry that you won't have enough options to choose from in light fixtures. There's practically an endless number of styles on the market to match every decor and catch everyone's imagination. The past few years have proved to be a lighting designer's dream as fixtures have become more decorative and lighting schemes more varied and eclectic. From nostalgic reproductions to architecturally inspired designs and contemporary styles, there are models to suit any look in the form of wall sconces, chandeliers, strip lights, recessed canister lights, track lights, ceiling fixtures, and novelty types. The copious selection of finishes in all of these styles offers lots of excitement, too. Look for everything from colored, enamels to brass, chrome, pewter, nickel, and copper, which can be brushed, matted, or antiqued. There are also vintage designs in wrought iron and verdigris. For more interest, select fixtures with a combination of finishes, such as a verdigris with antiqued brass or copper. Mix matte and polished finishes. But stick to a style that is compatible with other elements in the room's décor.

In a large room, combine more than one fixture type. In a bathroom, a ceiling fixture that includes a ventilating fan is especially practical. For accenting, pair uplighting fixtures, such as wall sconces, with downlighting types: recessed lights or a ceiling-mounted unit, for example. Install track lighting to wash an entire wall with illumination. Do this when you want to call attention to the architecture, a beautiful wallcovering, a special paint technique, or a mural. Experiment with light to create different shapes, patterns, and texture on a plain wall.

Finally, before you purchase a light fixture, ask to see it lit up in the store. That way you can be sure it produces the effect you desire. It's also a good idea to show the store's lighting specialist your plans and perhaps tile and paint samples so that he or she can guide you with your selection.

GENERAL RULES FOR LIGHTING A BATHROOM

In all but the tiniest of bathrooms, ceiling-mounted lamps are necessary for sufficient general illumination. A good choice is recessed lighting. How much you need, of course, depends on the size of the room. If it is less than 100 square feet, one fixture is sufficient. Add another fixture for each additional 50 square feet. If the surfaces around the room are light-absorbing dark hues, such as mahogany-stained cabinets, deep-colored walls, or black granite countertops, you may have to compensate with stronger lamps. If the bulbs you are using are not providing enough general light, you need to substitute them with ones that have more lumens. The next time you shop for bulbs, read the packaging, which indicates the lumens per watt (LPW) produced by a bulb.

Besides general illumination, recessed fixtures are ideal over a tub or shower area or in a toilet compartment. Some are designed specifically for damp locations, and a variety of trim is available to create different lighting effects, such as wall washing and accent lighting.

Opposite: *A custom-designed "shade," created with translucent-glass panels, diffuses the light cast by bright bulbs.*
Left: *Grooming tasks around this vanity area are enhanced by lamps that cast light with red and yellow overtones, which produce a flattering skin-tone effect.*

If fluorescent side lights are mandated by your local code, you'll be happy to know that they come with a special coating that reduces glare and diffuses the light to minimize shadows. Install them up to 48 inches apart for sufficient lighting, and supplement them with recessed or sur-face-mounted ceiling fixtures. Also, use the deluxe warm white fluorescent bulbs that more closely resemble natural light.

LIGHTING FOR MIRRORS

You'll need even, shadow-free lighting for applying makeup, shaving, or caring for hair. It should illuminate both sides of the face, under the chin, and the top of the head. Plan to use at least 120 incandescent watts. Never aim lighting into the mirror. Decorative sconces, installed face height, on either side of a small mirror do the job nicely. Place them no higher than 60 inches above the floor and at least 28 inches but not more than 60 inches apart, unless you pair them with anoth-er vanity light source. Ideally, combine wall sconces with a ceiling or wall-mounted fixture above the mirror.

Make sure the fluorescent fixture and lamps provide the best color rendering for makeup and realistic skin tone, within a range of 2,700K to 3,500K CCT. A large mirror, such as a three-way model used over a double vanity, will require a different approach. In such a case, treat each lavatory as a separate task area and light each portion of the vanity accordingly.

Depending on your design, you may want to install a series of side-light columns or span the entire mirrored wall with a fixture that integrates the entire sink/counter/

Right: *The lamp installed in the ceiling of the shower is rated for a damp location. For safety purposes, it is also out of reach.*

mirror area. Mount the fixtures 78 inches off the floor for the best results, per the recommended guidelines of the American Lighting Association.

Theatrical lighting strips are a great idea—if you install enough lamps. Too few very bright ones will create glare. Select units that use soft white lamps instead of clear globes or exposed bulbs. Because light is magnified by reflection in the mirror, cut glare by lowering the wattage; substitute 15-watt bulbs for ones that use 25 watts, for example.

Use a combination of both side and overhead theatrical strips so that individual bulb wattage can be lower. Add a dimmer switch so everyone in the house can adjust the light to his or her own needs. Recessed fixtures can be effective, especially incandescent fixtures with glass collars. Center them over the vanity countertop 36 to 48 inches apart.

SHOWER AND TUB LIGHTS

Light around the tub and shower area has to be bright enough for safety and grooming, adjusting water temperature or shower heads, and reading (if you care to read while you soak). Recessed downlights or any other fixtures designed for wet areas are fine. Shielded fixtures eliminate glare, and shatter-resistant white acrylic diffusers are the safest. Any light fixture installed in a wet or damp area has to be protected properly so that water cannot accumulate in wiring compartments, lamp holders, or other electrical parts. Your professional electrician will know how to handle the situation and can recommend the proper fixture.

CREATING ARCHITECTURAL EFFECTS WITH LIGHTING

Lighted coves, soffits (or cornices), and valances make the most of architectural features in a room. Fixtures designed for this purpose create dramatic reflective light. Coves distribute light upward. Soffits distribute light downward. Valances distribute light both up and down. A shield, such as molding, hides the light itself. Consider incorporating one of these ideas into your design if you want to make a big splash with the lighting in your bathroom or to create a focal point above a tub or vanity.

Be creative when thinking about architectural lighting. Install it along the top or bottom of cabinets or inside the cove of a raised ceiling. Integrate a lighted valance with a vaulted ceiling or a curtain sweep, install a small spotlight in a wall niche, highlight molding. Whatever you decide, first analyze your architectural lighting needs. Ask yourself these questions:

❦ Is the reflected wall or ceiling surface attractive enough to call attention to it?

❦ Can I alter the look of the lighting by tinting the color of the surface upon which it reflects?

❦ Can I increase lighting efficiency by painting the interior of the valance, cove, or soffit white? (Remember, light-colored surfaces are reflective.)

❦ Does the reflected light enhance the rest of the room's light?

❦ Is the ceiling high enough (at least 8 feet) to keep the light from spilling onto the walls? (The top of the cove should be at least 18 inches from the ceiling.)

These are the issues that will shape your ideas. Talk with your contractor to see what is feasible in your design. For real luxury, don't stop with a whirlpool; set a relaxing *mood.* If your bathroom is nondescript, if the fixtures and materials are plain standards, you can still find the necessary drama to make your bath unique and sophisticated by adding thoughtful lighting to your plan. You can create your own Garden of Eden with a few well-positioned plants and lights. Finally, your lighting scheme makes the biggest difference in the overall look and function of your bathroom. Plan wisely.

Opposite: *A strip of orange neon lights along the edge of the ceiling beams above the tub add a surprising dash of color.*
Above: *There are many reflective materials in this bathroom, including lots of glass and light-colored surfaces—even a copper shower. But properly shielded lamps never create glare in the room.*

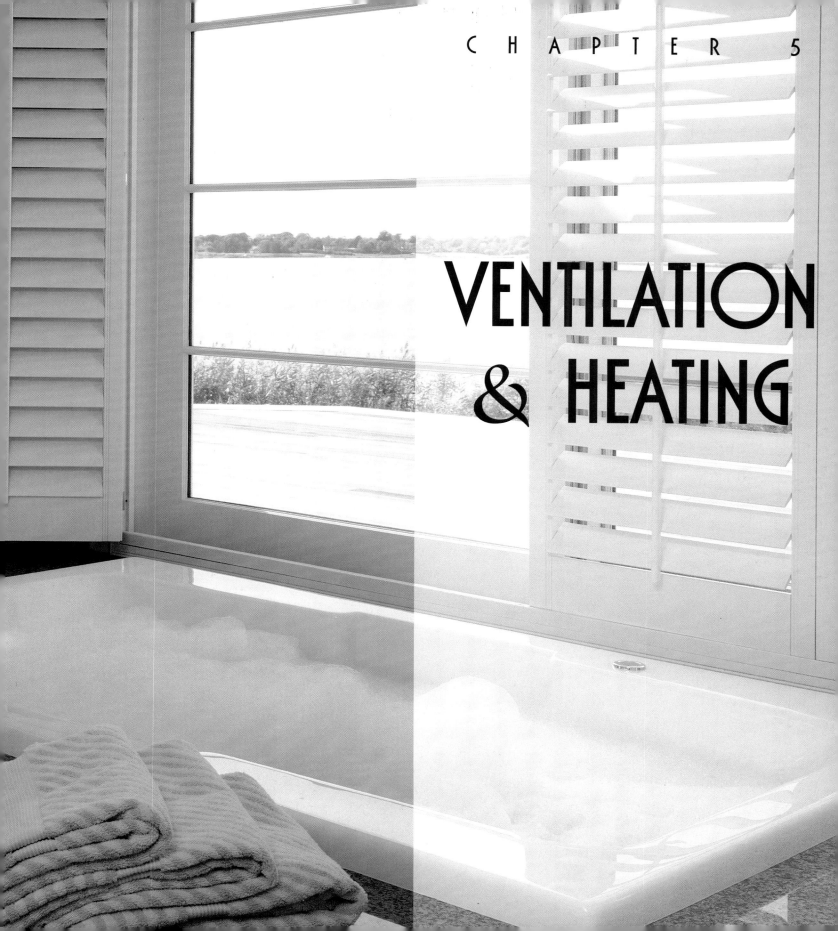

VENTILATION & HEATING

Foggy mirrors and cold floors are two of the quickest ways to get off to the wrong start in the morning. Especially when you can prevent both of them. All it takes is proper ventilation of your bathroom and sufficient heating.

Besides minor annoyances, however, there are larger issues that are affected by how much attention you pay to venting and heating the room: your health and comfort, as well as the prevention of moisture damage to the new bathroom itself.

VENTILATION

Adequate ventilation is a must in any humid environment, and you can't get much more humid than the modern bathroom retreat. Those fabulous home-spa features (multiple showerheads, rain bars, jetted tubs, and saunas) use more water than standard fixtures, raising the humidity level in the bathroom accordingly. The only solution is a good ventilation system.

Ventilation combats the steam and condensation that cause mildew, rot, and deterioration of the room's surfaces as well as the surrounding rooms or exterior walls of the house. If you haven't installed a proper moisture barrier between the bathroom and the exterior wall, besides peeling and chipping paint, you may face serious structural damage.

Previous page: *The window above the tub slides open and a smaller unit in the shower cranks out, for ventilation on demand.*
Below: *A tilt-out glass panel can be left open to release steam even when the shower door is closed.*
Opposite: *In this airy retreat conventional windows pair with an openable skylight for maximum comfort.*

Opposite: *Terra cotta tiles provide excellent conduction for radiant floor heat.*
Above: *A heated towel rack, a popular amenity in today's bath, easily plugs into the electrical outlet.*

If you install glossy ceramic tiles on bathroom surfaces, your ventilation needs are greater than if you use an absorbent material, such as cork. Unfortunately, many absorbent materials aren't appropriate for the bath because they mildew and spread bacteria. Even glossy paints can resist absorption and create moisture problems. Beyond concerns for bathroom surfaces and structural elements, imagine the air quality in a stuffy, unventilated bathroom. Noxious fumes released into the air by cleaning solutions and grooming products, including hair spray and nail polish, pose a health risk. The most common side effects of this indoor air pollution include eye, nose, and throat irritation. Not exactly the picture you had in mind when you dreamed of creating a relaxing, sybaritic haven in your new bathroom, right? Here's what you can do to ensure a fresh, healthy environment in the new bath.

ONE: *Incorporate a window into your design.* The simplest form of ventilation is natural: a window. If you don't have access to a window (for example, the bathroom is not located on an outside wall), investigate a vented sky-light or a roof window. Many come with electrically oper-ated controls for easy handling. In a multilevel house, you can even install a shaft or tunnel that makes it possible to bring light and air from an operable skylight or roof win-dow into a bathroom on the ground floor. Some of these units work by remote control for easy operation.

After you choose your windows and decide where they will work best, you may need additional measures to control glare, reduce winter heat loss, block unwanted summer heat, and create privacy—all while preserving the view out-side. This calls for flexible controls that respond to the time of day, season, and outside weather.

Window accessories take many forms: storm windows of glass or plastic that you add to inside or outside of the win-dow; awnings or shutters mounted on the outside; or pleat-

Smart Tip About Heating and Windows

If you have ever sat in a tub below a poorly insulated window on a January night, you know how unpleasant it can be to feel a steady stream of cold air wafting down on you. A well-designed window will inhibit heat loss in winter, as well as heat gain in summer. So, if you don't plan to exchange an old unit for something new and more efficient, think some more. Between 20 and 30 percent of a home's heat loss is through old windows. Today's windows are better sealed against leakage and better insulated against heat loss through the glass. If you can't enjoy that new soaking tub year-round, is it worth it?

Wherever you live, for a more comfortable and even tempera-ture in your new bath, consider replacing a less-efficient window with one that is protected with low-emissivity (low-E) coating and thermopane on the glass. For easy maintenance and opera-tion, choose a unit clad in aluminum or vinyl.

ed shades, blinds, and curtains mounted on the inside. Most window treatments can be adjusted, seasonally or daily.

Choose a window control system that will both enhance your comfort while in the bathroom and help create the design expression you are seeking. (See "Chapter Seven: Creating Style.") You can take your first cue from the cli-mate. Window treatments for a hot climate should block direct sunlight. In a cool climate, use insulated window treatments to block draft. Next consider privacy. If your bath window is vulnerable from the yard or neighboring house, choose a device that can be easily closed to block all views to the interior. Your final selection will have to accommodate the type and size of windows, the appear-ance you want and, of course, your budget. Here are a few of your choices.

❦ Storm Windows. If you live in a place with cold winters and are beginning with old leaky windows, you can either replace the windows with newer, more energy efficient win-dows or tighten them by caulking and weather stripping and adding a storm window to the inside or outside. Just make sure the storm window can be opened and closed without removing the entire unit, particularly if it is located above the ground story.

❦ Blinds. Adjustable blinds are a good way to control light glare and create privacy, though they don't add to the win-dow's energy efficiency. Two types of slatted blinds enable you to direct the sunlight where you want, while maintain-ing a view to the outdoors. Horizontal blinds made of alu-minum or vinyl slates are the best for south-facing win-dows because they can shut out the higher sunlight that comes from the south. They also ensure privacy. You can angle them upward, to let light in but prevent the view into the bathroom, or close them tight to completely block the light when it is too hot.

For windows on the east and west, vertical blinds work the best by blocking out the low-angle sun that adds so much heat on summer afternoons. Available in various tints, fab-rics, and widths, vertical blinds can be rotated to direct sunlight where you want it. They can be closed completely

Right: *This bathroom requires greater ventilation because glossy surfaces like ceramic tile and glass shower doors are nonabsorbant materials.*

or drawn open to the side of the window.

❧ Shades. Unlike blinds that contain slats to block out light when fully closed, some shades let in light even when closed. You can, however purchase sun-blocking shades, but they are higher priced. Beside standard roll-up shades, there are pleated and accordion styles, as well as Roman shades. In this moist room, make sure any fabric is treated for mildew resistance. Pleated shades stack rather than roll up, and ride down in tracks. Single-layer pleated shades fold like an accordion. Another type is made of two layers of fabric and forms a honey-comb shape when viewed from the side.

❧ Curtains. Curtains control glare and create privacy. But like fabric shades, bathroom curtains should be treated to mildew-cide—or, at least, be washable. You can purchase insulated curtains, but they are not washable. It's better to combine a washable curtain with an insulated shade or blind.

❧ Awnings and Shutters. Awnings can block direct sunlight from entering the window. They work best on south-facing openings, though. To keep late afternoon sunlight out of west-facing windows, you'll need awnings that lower to cover almost the full depth of the window. Shutter your bath windows only if you want to fit the other windows on the house, similarly; otherwise your bathroom windows will look out of place. For privacy, you may want to consider interior wood shutters instead of fabric window treatments. You can easily mount them to an entire window unit or the bottom half of a double- or single-hung window.

TWO: *Install a ventilation system.* In most jurisdictions, local building codes require fans in bathrooms that do not have windows. Even if you have access to natural ventilation, there are times you won't want to keep a window open (the middle of winter, for example). There are three types of bathroom ventilation systems for your consideration.

bathing. It is not the most effective option, but it is an inexpensive one because it doesn't involve ductwork. If ductwork is too expensive for your budget, consider installing a recirculating fan.

❧ A Ducted System. This type of ventilation system discharges humidity in the bathroom by removing moist, stale air and odors and venting them through ductwork to the outdoors. If the unit is properly sealed, it will not bring outside air indoors. It simply clears the room of bad air and allows fresh air from the rest of the house to circulate into the bathroom.

Sometimes, these fans are vented into the attic. This is not recommended because of the potential for causing moisture damage under the attic eaves.

Some of the latest options offered by manufacturers of bathroom fans include remote-location units, built-in lighting, units that include heaters, multiple speeds, quiet operation, and an automatic-on feature that is triggered by a device that senses high levels of humidity.

❧ A Recirculating Fan. As its name implies, this type of fan simply moves the air around in the room. It does not vent air to the outdoors, but it does help to dispel some of the moisture that has accumulated on surfaces during

❧ Room Exhaust Fans. Separate exhaust fans mount anywhere on a ceiling or outer wall of a new bathroom. The main thing is to connect the fan to the outside via a vent cap on the roof or sidewall. To match the fan capacity to the room size, divide the volume of the room by 7.5. For example, if you are adding a new bathroom measuring 7 by 9 feet with an 8-foot ceiling, its volume is 504 cubic feet. The proper-size fan will have a capacity of 504 divided by 7.5 or 67.2 cubic feet per minute (cfm). Exhaust fans vary between 75 to 600 cfm, so the smallest one would suffice. Noise is another issue when shopping for exhaust fans. Fan noise is rated in sones. The quietest bath exhaust fans come in at around 1 sone—about the level of a refrigerator fan. Fans can be rated as high as 4 sones.

HEATING

Something that is often neglected in design is sufficient heating. This often happens when a room is added on to accommodate another bath. The capacity of the current heating system may not be adequate to serve the new space efficiently. For your own comfort, therefore, check the heat load capacity of your furnace. Your local utility company may be able to assist you in this matter, or call in a heating specialist for professional advice.

Unless you're adding on a lot of extra space to the house, you won't have to replace your heating system (although if it is old and burns a lot of energy, it may be a good time to replace it with a more efficient model). Often you can supplement the existing system with alternative sources of heat. Some of your choices include:

❦ Radiant Floor Heat. Energy-efficient, invisible, and space-saving (no radiators or baseboard heaters to take up valuable floor space) radiant heating is a trend that is growing in popularity. The system uses hot water or electric wire coils installed underneath the floor. As the floor warms up, the heat rises to take the chill out of the rest of the room. This may be a viable option if you are replacing a floor or building from scratch. However, some flooring types may be incompatible with this type of heat. Good candidates include ceramic tile, slate, and wood.

❦ Towel Warmers. Imagine wrapping yourself in a toasty towel to ease the transition from steamy shower to cool room. In the past, this is the kind of "luxury" item you may have associated with a first-class hotel, but towel warmers are becoming more standard fare in residential design, particularly in master suites. There are two types: traditional hydronic radiator-compatible models and that work on electricity and simply plug into a wall socket. Look for a growing variety of styles, colors, and shapes to coordinate with many décors.

❦ Toespace Heaters. Another amenity growing in popularity—especially in master baths and children's bathrooms—toespace heaters fit neatly into deadspace under a vanity cabinet. They provide a pleasant blast of warm air on demand. Just flip the switch to turn cold tile floors toasty. Although electric heat sources can be expensive compared to other types, these devices aren't meant for constant use. In the long run, they shouldn't add too much to your energy bills.

❦ Heat Lamps. These devices use infrared bulbs that radiate heat into the space. Heat lamps are usually mounted in the ceiling around the tub or outside the shower area. In most cases, they are monitored by a timer.

❦ Convection Heaters. A convection heater warms the air, then circulates it using a small fan that is built into the unit. For an easy convection heat source, install an electric heater on the bathroom wall or ceiling. Many models also come with exhaust fans and lights to combine ventilation and heating. Other forms of convection heat sources include gas heaters, which are available for propane or natural gas and heat pumps. If you choose a gas heater, always properly vent it to the exterior of the house.

CHAPTER 6

SELECTING PRODUCTS & MATERIALS

The products you select to outfit your new bathroom will affect both your design and your budget. If you choose top-of-the-line products, expect a top-of-the-line bill. Factors that influence the cost of new fixtures, cabinetry, countertops, and flooring include updated technology and type of finish. The smarter the device, the more you'll pay for it. Likewise, the fancier the finish, the higher the price tag. But cost does not always reflect quality, nor does it equate necessarily with satisfaction. And quality and personal satisfaction are the most important factors to consider when making any product selection.

So, how can you make smart choices about items like tubs and showers, tile, and cabinets? How can you tell whether a product is reliable and will endure the daily abuse of water and moisture? Are there basic differences that make one faucet or a particular toilet better than another? To find out, you can do a little research. Shop around. Visit bath designer showrooms, read books, and don't be afraid to ask questions. Otherwise, you can take your chances. If you're not the gambling type, however, here are some steps you can take to select products and materials for your new bath with confidence.

Previous page: *A hammered-metal basin pairs with acrylic and chrome fittings.*
Left: *This glazed washing basin is mounted on top of the counter.*
Right: *A protective urethane finish makes wood a stylish surface option.*

SMART STEPS

ONE: ***Separate the product from the hype.*** A high price does not always mean high quality. Find out what is different about a toilet that costs $100, for example, and one that sells for $300 or even $1,000. This way you can decide whether the higher price is worth it. A knowledgeable salesperson will be able to tell you. If not, contact the manufacturer. Many have 800 numbers and Web sites set up to handle consumer questions. Sometimes the price hike is because of a feature you can't see. For example, a faucet with replaceable parts costs much more than a new faucet with parts that cannot be replaced. How much do you want to gamble that the faucet you buy won't break?

TWO: ***Weigh your options.*** Analyze the benefits and the risks that come with each product. Once you have that information, a decision will be easier. If you are sprucing up an old bath or adding a new one in a house you expect to sell soon, you might install a less-expensive countertop material, for example. But if you are making a major investment in a remodeling project that you plan to live with for a long time, you might be happier in the long run with something that may cost more but gives you greater satisfaction and will be more reliable for years to come.

THREE: ***Seek reliable advice.*** Ask the manufacturer about the expected life of the product or its efficiency. Don't take advice from a store clerk if he or she is not an experienced remodeling professional. Talk to your contractor, who may be familiar with the product or can pass along critical feedback from other clients who may have purchased the same item or something similar to it.

FOUR: ***Don't make a choice based on style or color.*** It doesn't work for cars, and it won't work for building materials. Sure, style and color are important, but it's just as easy to find a first-rate fixture that looks great in your new bathroom as it is to find one that looks fabulous but performs poorly. Opt for quality.

Above: *A sculptured pedestal sink, mounted into a wall recess, almost becomes part of the architecture in this powder room.*
Opposite: *The rich marble platform and neoclassical columns provide a suitable setting for a glamorous jetted tub for two.*

FIVE: *Be wary of some handmade products for the bath.* You may be tempted by a handsome unglazed sink from a chic pottery shop. Certainly, it will add a unique cachet to your design, but an unglazed sink may not meet local code. Don't buy on impulse before checking out the building codes in your area. If there's any doubt in your mind, ask if you can leave a refundable deposit on the item, and then speak with your contractor, who should be familiar with the rules.

SIX: *Prorate costs.* You may be dismayed by the initial sticker price, but when you divide the cost of the product or material by its anticipated longevity (how many years you expect it to last), you may be amazed at how reasonable it really is. Of course, this won't alleviate an immediate cash-flow problem, but it will ease some of the sticker shock. An expensive product that will last for 20 years may be a better choice than a cheaper one that may have to be replaced in five years. Again, weigh that decision against how long you plan to stay in the house. Are the extra benefits worth it?

SEVEN: *Inquire about guarantees and service options.* Some offers are definitely better than others. Look at the warranties that come from the manufacturer, as well as those offered by the place of purchase. A store may offer immediate replacement of the entire unit. While this may sound great, it isn't if you have to pay for labor or schedule time off from work for the removal and reinstallation of a fixture. Find out whether there is a better way. If all that is wrong with a faucet is a faulty washer, you may not want to yank out the entire unit. It should be your call. Find a place that offers a warranty based on the problems with the product. And always get written copies of all warranties from the store or your contractor.

EIGHT: *Do a reality check.* Look at your situation, and choose the best products and materials for the way you live. Don't get swept away by bells and whistles that can blow your budget. Your bottom line isn't bottomless, so compare each extra-cost feature with your real needs and lifestyle. A sumptuous shower with 18 massaging hydrojets may be your fantasy, but if your morning routine is a race against the clock to get to work on time, invest the extra money elsewhere. Besides, multiple shower outlets, as well as large tubs, may require larger water-supply lines, and that might not be an option.

NINE: *Leave nothing to chance.* Investigate every option and every detail for the new bathroom. Don't find yourself bemoaning what you should have done when it's too late. After you sign the final check is not the time to realize you could have installed an in-line heater to keep bath water consistently warm or a steam unit in the shower. Discover everything that's out there—before getting started. Don't

miss any of the fun stuff, and you won't have any regrets or extra charges for changes made after work has begun.

Although the trend in recent years has been to increase the size of the bathroom, most are still relatively small compared with other rooms in the house. Yet this room remains the most expensive per square foot to renovate. This behooves you to invest wisely.

FIXTURES AND FITTINGS

Thirty years ago, items like tubs, toilets, and sinks were standard fare, not to mention boring. Who could have imagined they would generate the excitement they do today? As bathrooms have been elevated to symbolize status in American homes over the last couple of decades,

second only in prestige to kitchens, even the most pragmatic items have become elements of design. But in addition to appearance, the workings of bathroom fixtures have become technologically more glamorous, as well.

TUBS

Soakers, whirlpools, classic claw-footed models, tubs for two, spas for four, contoured shapes, ovals, squares, or rounded tubs, streamlined or sculptured models, tubs with neck rests and arm rests. Tubs in a variety of colors. Freestanding tubs. Tubs set into platforms. Tubs you step down into. It's your soak, so have it your way.

Ask yourself: How do I like to bathe? Do I prefer a long, lingering soak or an invigorating hydromassage? A popular trend is the sunk-in whirlpool tub, which comes with an array of therapeutic and relaxing options in the form of neck jets, back jets, side jets, multiple jets, or single jets that are installed in the walls behind the tub. Generally, tubs are made of one of the three following materials:

❦ Fiberglass. Lightweight and moldable, a fiberglass tub is the least expensive type you can buy. But it's prone to scratching and wear after about a dozen years. Some come with an acrylic finish, which holds up against wear longer.

❦ Solid Acrylic. A mid-price-range product, it is more durable than fiberglass and less prone to scratching because the color is solid all the way through. Whirlpool tubs are usually made of acrylic because it can be shaped easily. It's also lightweight, an important feature for large tubs that can put damaging stress on structural elements under the floor.

❦ Cast Iron. An enamel-coated, cast iron tub will endure as long as your house stands. It's a heavyweight, though, and not recommended for a large soaking tub.

The most common size for a tub that backs up against a wall is 32x60 inches, but you can find models in widths of 24 to 42 inches. If someone in the family is tall, no problem: You can purchase a standard tub that's up to 72 inches long.

SHOWERS

Spectacular spray options and spa features make showering as sybaritic as the most luxuriously appointed bath. Shower

units separate from bathtubs can be prefabricated from molded fiberglass or acrylic. They come in widths of 32, 36, and 48 inches, with a standard depth of 36 inches and a height of 73 inches. Custom-built showers are typically constructed of solid-surfacing, ceramic tile, or stone. Top-of-the-line features include massaging hydrotherapy sprays, steam units, a foot whirlpool, built-in seating and storage, even a CD player. Amazing technology lets you enjoy a full body massage on a miserly amount of water. Although by law new shower heads may not deliver more than 2.5 gallons of water per minute, you can install as many as you wish.

The only thing limiting your shower is your imagination and your budget. If you want it, it's out there. Unless you're interested in a strictly no-frills unit, think about installing more than one shower head and mixing and matching devices from any or all of the following three basic spray categories.

❧ Fixed Spray. This type is mounted on the wall or ceiling, and it may or may not come with a massage option. New versions include a device that propels water into the air to give you a hydromassage. Other nifty models, called rain bars, let you close your eyes and pretend you're in a rain forest where gentle mists pamper you with a soft rinse. Or you can opt for a cascade of water that is delivered by a waterfall spout.

❧ Hand-held Spray. A hand-held device is convenient for directing water where you want it. It stores in a wall-mounted slide bar and can be adjusted up and down to accommodate the tallest or shortest bather. Combine a hand-held spray with a stationary shower head, and add a massager with as many as eight settings and a body brush, and you've created a custom shower environment that rivals any first-class away-from-home spa.

Left: *A custom system that includes a fixed shower head and a hand-held spray, as well as a preset temperature valve, offers a perfect shower.*

❧ Jet Sprays. Just like those used in whirlpool tubs, these sprays are housed behind the shower walls. One manufacturer offers as many as 16 with its shower unit. Jet sprays can be programmed to various settings. Get a therapeutic hydromassage to relax stiff neck muscles or a sore back, for example. If you like, select a full body massage at whatever intensity is comfortable for you.

TOILETS

Believe it or not, you do have choices when selecting a toilet for your new bathroom. Vitreous china is still the material of preference, but there's a wide range of colors and style options to suit contemporary or traditional tastes. If you like something sleek, select a European-inspired elongated bowl. Though toilet sizes vary somewhat among manufacturers, an elongated bowl will extend about 2 inches more into the room than a standard version. The typical height of a toilet seat is 15 inches, but some come as high as 18 inches, which can be more comfortable for tall or older persons.

Another option is whether your new toilet will be a one-piece, low-profile model or a two-piece unit. There are style variations within both types, including rounded bowls, long square shapes, and vintage looks. Nostalgia lovers will be happy to know that Victorian-style high-tank toilets are still manufactured. Scaled-down toilets are available, too, for condos and apartments short on space or for tiny powder rooms, such as those tucked into a stairwell.

If you are still fighting in your household about whether the seat should be kept up or down, give peace a chance. Look into these new gender-friendly features: a lid that automatically lowers when the toilet is flushed or the toilet that shines a red light in the bowl when the seat is up and a green light when the lid is down.

If that isn't enough, consider a residential urinal. One type fits into the wall like a built-in laundry hamper; another sits on the floor next to the toilet.

Besides style and type, you should be concerned about the flushing mechanism. Although appearance factors can affect cost (low-profile, one-piece, and elongated bowls being at least twice the price of standard two-piece models),

Left: *A sleek low-profile toilet looks contemporary in this bathroom. It's low-flush feature uses less than one-fourth the amount of water used by older toilets.*
Opposite: *This reproduction sink and its fittings suit the room's Victorian style.*

the flushing mechanism may have an even bigger impact on the price tag. New toilets must conform to the government's low-flush standard, which mandates that no more than 1.6 gallons of water be used per flush. But that may change due to complaints about effectiveness. Manufacturers are working to improve flushing mechanisms. In the meantime, Congress may relax standards slightly.

There are three basic types of flushing mechanisms, listed in order of their cost, starting with the least expensive.

❧ Gravity-fed. This is the standard device used by two-piece toilets. Press down the lever, and the force of the water that is released from the tank and into the bowl flushes waste down the drain and out through the pipes.

❦ Pressure-assisted. With this flushing mechanism, water pressure in the line compresses air and, using a small amount of water, forces the bowl to empty.

❦ Electric Pump. In this system, a small electric pump quietly pushes water and waste through the toilet. This is much less common than the preceding two methods.

Manufacturers are also working on vacuum-flush toilets that would operate similarly to those on airlines, and uses a miniscule amount of water. However, this type of toilet is still in the development phase and is not ready for the residential market.

BIDETS

A standard fixture in European bathrooms for decades bidets have been slow to catch on in the American market. They are gaining in popularity, however, particularly in new construction and high-end remodeling where they are

becoming status symbols in master suites. Typically a bidet is selected to match the toilet, and the fixtures are installed side by side.

LAVATORIES

You may find it practically impossible to select one lavatory over another because they come in so many sizes, shapes, styles, and colors. Sensuous curves, sculpted bowls, and beautiful, durable finishes can make this vessel a work of art—and an important element in your overall design. Today's lav can be made of vitreous china, cast iron, enameled steel, fiberglass, acrylic (solid-surfacing material), stone, faux stone, or metal. Its finish may be hand painted, contoured, beveled, brushed, or polished. A sink can be a freestanding pedestal or it can be mounted to the wall or be part of a vanity top.

Vanity sinks, in pairs or as a single lav, are designed to be installed in one of four ways:

❧ Self-rimming. This type of sink is surface-mounted. The bowl drops into the counter while the ridge forms a seal with the countertop surface. This ridge or rim can be decoratively carved or handpainted.

❧ Under-mounted. If you want a tailored look, an under-mounted sink may be for you. In this instance, the bowl is attached underneath the countertop for a clean, uncluttered appearance.

❧ Integral. As the word "integral" implies, the sink and countertop are fabricated from the same material—stone, faux stone, or solid-surfacing. The look is sleek, seamless, and sculptural.

❧ Rimmed. Unlike a self-rimming sink, a rimmed model requires a metal strip to form the seal between the top of the sink and the countertop.

There are attractive, shapely lavs in every price range. Colored lavatories are usually a bit pricier, as are delicate hand-painted designs. If you will do anything at the sink besides washing your hands and face and brushing your teeth, consider choices in design and size carefully before you buy.

Something that is too shallow, for example, may not be practical for rinsing hair or hand washables. A pedestal sink may be pretty, but if you apply makeup, style your hair, or shave, this type may not provide surface storage for related grooming items. Think before acting.

FAUCETS AND OTHER FITTINGS

Like showers, faucets are no longer just conduits of water. Today's faucet technology gives you much more control over your water. You can program an instrument for a pulsating effect or select the gentler rhythm of a babbling brook or a cascading waterfall; preset water temperature; enjoy a hot bath that never gets cold; protect children from scalding.

For quality, inquire about the materials used for the faucet's innards. The best choices are solid brass or a brass-base metal, which are corrosion-resistant. Avoid plastic—it won't hold up. Inquire about the faucet's valving, too. Many

faucets come with a washerless ceramic or nylon cartridge that lasts longer and is less prone to leaks. Ceramic is the better choice. Select finishes depending on your taste and other elements in the room that you may wish to coordinate with the fittings. Finishes include chrome, polished brass, enamel-coated colors, pewter, nickel, gold, and gold-plated.

Make a fashion statement by mixing finishes or selecting a design with inlaid stones or gems. Think of faucets as jewel-

Left: *For an ultimately soothing bath experience, this tub's spout has a waterfall effect.*
Right: *The new technology used to finish this widespread faucet set will maintain the polish-brass shine for years.*

ry for your bathroom, and accessorize accordingly. There are three basic types of faucets for your consideration:

❦ Center Set. This type has two separate valves (one for hot, another for cold) and a spout that are connected in one unit.

❦ Widespread. This type features a spout with separate hot- and cold-water valves. All appear to be completely separate pieces.

❦ Single Lever. This type has a spout and a single lever in one piece for one-hand control.

Whatever your decorating motif, you can find faucets to coordinate with the look you wish to achieve. Reproduction styles in brushed-metal finishes look good in traditional décors, as do graceful gooseneck spouts. Sleek geometrical shapes with enameled or high-gloss finishes enhance contemporary designs. And don't forget baubles. Stone, faux stone, or faux gem inserts on handles provide rich-looking details in strong architecturally inspired designs.

While you're admiring all the handsome faucet styles on today's market, remember function. Cross handles are charming, but they can be difficult to grasp for the elderly, disabled persons, or the very young. Levers and wrist

blades make more sense in these cases. If you like the simplicity of a single-lever faucet, install one with a hot-limit valve so that kids can't scald themselves.

GRAB BARS AND TOWEL BARS

The first thing to remember is that grab bars and towel bars are not interchangeable items. A grab bar must be installed so that it securely attaches to wall studs or blocking behind a shower or bathtub or at the toilet. For quality, shop for grab bars made of solid brass. For style, coordinate them with other hardware, such as the towel bars, faucets, and cabinet pulls and handles.

Like faucets, towel bars can be likened to jewelry for the bath. Don't skimp on this detail; look for ones with match-

ing toilet paper holders and door and wall hooks. Shop for quality brass or chrome construction with a finish that won't rust or tarnish when exposed to moisture.

STORAGE

Undoubtedly, an important aspect of your new bath's design is storage. Besides toiletries, grooming aids, extra linens, a hamper, and cleaning supplies, you may want to store gym equipment, books, magazines, and CDs, particularly if the room will be a place you can retreat to for adult quiet time after a day at work or with the kids.

No matter what the size of the bathroom is, it should contain a reasonable amount of storage. To get it, you'll have

Opposite: An updated version of an old-fashioned wall-mounted faucet looks sleek paired with an above-the-counter lav.
Right: *Custom-built open shelving provides storage for towels and toiletries and offers display space for plants and accessories.*

to thoroughly analyze the space and prioritize what items you must have handy, as well as any extras you'd like. Believe it or not, even a tiny 5x7-foot bathroom can accommodate spare rolls of toilet paper, additional bars of soap, a blow dryer, and curling iron, as well as a stack of clean towels, as long as you think storage issues through at the design stage of the project.

If you are working with a professional, he or she will have more than a few storage tricks to offer if you are specific about what you need. Is a vanity sufficient? Will it be for one or two persons? Do you require a medicine cabinet? How about a linen closet? Extra shelves? Drawers?

When you are acting on your own, go back to "Chapter Two, Function: Up Close and Personal," and review the questions about how you intend to use the new bath. Make a list of everything you want at hand. Scale back if necessary, but start big. For example, if your children will bathe in this room, include storage for bath toys—ideally, someplace other than

Smart Tips For Storage

A linen closet inside the bathroom is an amenity some homeowners think they can't afford if the space is small. If that's your dilemma, a little rethinking and reshuffling may yield the necessary room you thought you didn't have. First, reconsider the size of the bathroom fixtures you've been planning for your design. Would a smaller tub, shower unit, or vanity relieve the crunch? Second, think about building the closet into an adjoining room, if possible. Your designer may have other ideas, too.

You can't go wrong if you make good use of even the smallest pocket of space, like the toe-kick area at the bottom of the vanity, where you can install extra drawers or a slide-out step for kids who can't reach the sink yet. If there's a low-profile toilet next to the vanity, extend the countertop over the toilet. Ask your builder to suspend a drawer from underneath the extension. Don't forget to include a built-in shelf inside the shower or tub enclosure to hold soaps and shampoos. Use the wall space; install open shelves for extra towels, bars of soap, bubble bath, and the like. Better yet, think about opening up a wall between two studs and using the dead space for recessed shelving. One caution: Just don't cut the studs in case it is a load-bearing wall.

along the ledge of the tub. If you'll shave, groom your hair, or apply makeup at the vanity, pencil in a place—not the countertop—to keep essentials away from the sink and protected against exposure to water or dampness. If you're tired of toting dirty clothes downstairs to the basement or ground-floor laundry room, see whether your plan can accommodate a compact washer/dryer. These are just a few of the storage-related issues that could affect your project.

In any event, it's likely that you'll want at least a vanity and a medicine cabinet in your new bath. Like fixtures and fittings, they make important statements about how the new space will look, as well as how it will function.

VANITIES
Today there are many creative ways to approach the vanity. One is to treat the vanity as a decorative receptacle for a drop-in sink with just a countertop and legs, and no attached cabinetry. If you can sacrifice the storage a cabinet provides, this option will add drama to your design, especially if the countertop is outfitted with handsome tile,

Above: *A charming old cupboard puts colorful towels on display in a bathroom with vintage style.*
Opposite: *A custom-painted design and hand-crafted details distinguish this furniture vanity.*

stone, or colored concrete. But if you're limited by space and have to make the most of every inch, a vanity cabinet is the wisest choice. Cabinets are available in three ways:

🌣 Stock. Factory-made in a range of standard heights, sizes, and finishes, stock vanities are usually but not always the most economical type. Styles are limited.

🌣 Semi-custom. Factory-made and outfitted with custom options upon your order—and usually midrange in price—semi-custom vanities include extras such as pull-out bins, spin-out trays, special door styles, or custom finishes.

🌣 Custom. Built-to-order to your bathroom's specifications, custom vanity cabinets can be designed by your architect, interior designer, or designer/builder. This is typically, but not always the most expensive option.

A popular vanity trend is to retrofit a piece of fine wood furniture, such as an antique chest, with a lav, reproduction fittings, and an elegant countertop. But the wood surface has to be sealed with a protective coating that resists water and mildew. If you don't have the right piece of old furniture but want the same look, check out the new cabinet styles offered by manufacturers today. Look at designs created for the kitchen as well as the bath. Some are interchangeable and display furniture details. Fluted pilasters, elegant moldings, and filigree patterns adorn many models that also come with beautiful hardware and finishes engineered to hold up to humidity and mildew. They wipe clean easily, too, so you don't have to worry about upkeep.

Whether you select a vanity style that is traditional or contemporary, with a plastic laminate, metal, or wood finish, give the vanity cabinet as much consideration as you would if it were meant for the kitchen. Top-of-the-line solid-wood construction may be too expensive for most budgets. However, a sturdy plywood frame combined with dovetail and mortise-and tenon joinery is excellent, too. Make sure the interiors are well finished, however, and shelves aren't flimsy.

There are basically two construction styles for stock and semi-custom cabinetry: framed and frameless. Both are available from American manufacturers.

🌣 Framed. Framed cabinets feature a full frame across the face of the unit. Hinges may or may not be visible around doors and drawers.

🌣 Frameless. Frameless cabinets, often called European-style cabinets, are built without a face frame and therefore have a sleek appearance. Because the doors are mounted on the face of the box or are set into it, hinges are typically hidden inside.

MEDICINE CABINETS

You can find attractive medicine cabinets that can be wall-mounted or recessed into a nonload-bearing wall between the studs. From ultra contemporary visions in glass and lights to designs that make bold architectural statements, there's a wide selection of stock units to match any décor or cabinet style.

When shopping for a medicine cabinet, look for one that offers room for everything from toothbrushes to shaving cream and band aids. Choose one that spans the width of your vanity or beyond it, if wall space allows. In other words, buy the largest one you can find! Look for deep shelves that accommodate objects larger than a small pill bottle. Built-in lighting, swing-out mirrors, and three-way mirrored doors are some of the other extras you may want in a medicine cabinet. In addition, some units come with a lock or a separate compartment that can be locked to keep potentially dangerous substances out of the hands of young children.

SURFACING MATERIALS

Even in well-ventilated bathrooms, steam and moisture can take their toll. So it's important to select materials for the walls, floor, and countertop that can hold up to water. Plastic laminate and vinyl are good choices that come in different price ranges, depending on quality. Generally they are the most affordable. Ceramic tile, solid-surfacing materials, and concrete fall into the middle to high end of the spectrum. Installation and finishing techniques affect their costs. Natural stone, such as slate, granite, and marble, are at the high end of the price scale.

LAMINATE

Consider laminate for your bathroom countertops and flooring. When installed on counters, plastic laminate resists moisture superbly and is easy to maintain. It comes in so many colors, patterns, and textures that finding one to coordinate with other elements in your design—fixtures, tile, wallcovering—is easy. Want a countertop made of slate or marble, but can't afford the real thing? Does a

Above: *A mirrored door conceals a medicine cabinet that is part of a bank of storage built to this bath's specifications.*
Right: *One of the benefits of solid-surfacing materials is their potential for creating carved or beveled effects.*

buttery leather, smooth suede, cool glass, or warm wood appeal to you? A faux version in laminate may be the answer. Besides giving you a price break, plastic laminate offers a practical alternative to some natural materials that would be too delicate for such an installation. In that sense, it is a versatile and practical. Plastic laminate countertop material comes in various grades. It is generally affordable, so don't skimp by purchasing the cheapest one you can find. To get your money's worth, select the highest quality, which won't chip easily and stays looking good longer. At the very top of the line is "color-through" laminate. As opposed to laminate with color on the surface only, this type will not show a brown seam line at the edge because color is solid all the way through.

With regard to flooring, the latest laminate products boast easy care, as well as moisture and stain resistance. Manufacturers now offer literally dozens of designs that are dead ringers for real wood or stone. These come in either tongue-and-groove planks or as tiles. Like sheet laminate used for countertops, laminate flooring is more economical than the natural materials it portrays, and in most cases it installs right over old flooring.

Above: *Mixing raised-pattern, hand-painted, and roped accent strip tiles adds a three-dimensional look to a countertop design.*
Opposite: *A lively vinyl pattern on the floor perks up a plain room. It has the look of a pricier tile installation.*

VINYL

Textured vinyl flooring is an excellent choice for a bathroom designed for children or elderly people because it is the most slip-resistant material you can install. (If it isn't textured, however, it can be slippery when wet.) You don't have to sacrifice style for safety, either. Manufacturers have developed an extensive array of colors, patterns, and textures from which to choose. Unless you buy the highest grade, vinyl is the least expensive flooring on the market. Keep in mind, though, that inexpensive vinyl products tend to crack and tear even under normal use, and the finish wears off easily. For durability, you'll have to pay for a higher quality.

CERAMIC TILE

Besides its practical attributes, such as imperviousness to water, durability, and easy maintenance, ceramic tile offers the greatest opportunity to bring style and personality to your bathroom. Use it to add color, pattern, and texture to the wall, floor, or countertop. Enclose a tub or shower with it. Tile is versatile. It comes in a variety of shapes, sizes, and finishes. Use decorative tiles with hand-painted finishes or raised-relief designs to create a mural or mosaic. You're only limited by your imagination. Hand-painted tile is expensive, but it allows you to do something truly unique. If cost is a factor, accent standard tiles with a few hand-painted designs. Or achieve a similar look at less cost by using mass-produced tiles with silk-screened designs. Visit a tile showroom in your area or the design department of a nearby home center to get ideas. Mix and match embossed tiles, accent and trim strips, edges, and a contrasting colored grout (the compound that fills the joints). For long-lasting wear and easy maintenance,

Above: *Marble surfaces, such as this vanity top, are hard but porous. They require sealing to protect them from stain-damaging spills.*
Opposite: *Prefabricated cabinetry and a laminate countertop offer beauty without lots of maintenance.*

always apply a grout sealer in areas exposed to water, such as the countertop or tub surround.

Consider the finish when you're shopping for tile. There are two kinds: glazed and unglazed. Unglazed tiles are not sealed and always come in a matte finish. If you want to use them in the bathroom, you will have to apply a sealant. Glazed tiles are coated with a sealant that makes them impervious to water. This glaze can be matte finished or one that is highly polished. Highly glazed tile, however, can be a hazard on the floor. Instead, opt for a soft-glazed tile intend-ed for floor installation. When shopping, inquire about the manufacturer's slip-resistance rating for the tile you are considering. It's also a good idea to make sure any tile selected for a countertop installation can handle the spills and knocks that occur typically around the sink and on the countertop surface.

SOLID-SURFACING MATERIAL

An extremely durable, easily maintained synthetic made of polyester or acrylic, solid-surfacing material is used to fabricate countertops, sinks, shower enclosures, and floors. It's not cheap, costing almost as much per linear foot as granite or marble, but it wears long and well. It is completely impervious to water, and any dents or abrasions that may occur over time are repaired easily with a light sanding. At first, solid surfacing was available only in shades of white or pastel colors, but now its color palette has greatly expanded and includes faux-stone finishes, as well.

STONE AND CONCRETE

Granite, marble, and slate are probably the most expensive materials you can choose for a floor or countertop. They are all extremely durable and rich looking. Two other stone materials, limestone and concrete, are finding their way into the creative hands of designers today, too. Unlike granite, marble, and slate, limestone has more of a primitive, textured appeal. Concrete offers flexibility. It can be colored, shaped, carved, and inlaid with objects like pieces of tile for a sophisticated effect. Concrete offers lots of new creative possibilities, but it cracks very easily.

When considering any one of these options for flooring, however, remember that they are cold underfoot and unforgiving—anything you drop that is delicate will break. Stone may pose a safety hazard on the floor, too, because it gets slick when wet. A fall on a stone floor can cause serious injury. Older persons and children are at particular risk. If you choose one of these materials, use slip-resistant carpeting over it.

As countertop material, any one of these materials introduces a dramatic element to the room. The only thing you have to worry about is sealing your natural countertop properly against moisture.

These materials are also heavy, so beware if you plan to use them on a floor or to fabricate a tub or shower. Check with your builder or a structural engineer to find out whether you'll need additional support under the floor to carry the extra weight.

WOOD

Wood has typically been taboo in the bathroom because of its susceptibility to water damage, mildew, and warping. However, if you seal it properly with one of today's sophisticated, high-tech finishes you can use it safely. This should come as good news to homeowners who like the incomparable warmth offered by real wood. On the floor, walls, or countertop, wood requires a urethane finish. Some kinds of wood, such as teak, hold up better than other softer porous types like pine.

PRODUCT SHOPPING LIST

It's a good idea to keep a record of what products you are buying for the new bath, what they cost, plus each one's style name or number, size, color, quantity, and the manu-facturer's name, plus the cost. To make that task simple, here's a list of the typical purchases involved in a new bath. You can use the list to do your shopping and to keep a permanent record of your expenditures.

Description	Style	Size	Color	Qty.	Mfr.	Total Price
Permanent Fixtures						
Bidet						
Door						
Pedestal lavatory						
Shower door (if separate)						
Shower stall						
Standard tub						
Toilet						
Vanity lavatory						
Whirlpool tub						
Window						
Fittings						
Grab bars						
Hand-held sprayers						
Lavatory faucet set						
Shower curtain rod						
Soap dish						
Standard towel bars						
Shower faucet set						
Toilet-paper holder						
Toothbrush holder						
Tub faucet set						

Description	Style	Size	Color	Qty.	Mfr.	Total Price
Storage						
Cabinets						
Medicine cabinet						
Open shelves						
Vanity						
Surfacing products						
Countertop						
Floor tile						
Other flooring						
Paint						
Wall tile						
Paneling						
Wainscot						
Wallpaper						
Lighting and electrical						
Ceiling fixtures						
Exhaust fan						
Exhaust fan with light						
Fluorescent strips						
Heat lamp						
Heated towel bars						
Mini light strips						
Mini spotlights						
Miscellaneous						
Recessed canisters						
Track lights						
Wall sconces						

CHAPTER 7

CREATING STYLE

Today's bathrooms have style and personality. Whether yours comes together with the help of a team of professionals or through your own efforts, it should say something about you. Is your favorite color purple? Are you crazy for Art Deco? Are you a country lover, a city slicker, or a traditionalist at heart? Approach this phase of the process with as much creative abandon as you can muster.

Favorite decorating themes or looks that you've incorporated into other rooms in the house can be carried over into the bath, if you like, using color, pattern, texture, and finishing materials that unify the overall décor. In this chapter, you'll get some ideas about identifying what style is right for you and how to pull all the elements together seamlessly into one coordinated scheme.

DEFINING YOUR STYLE

Before locking yourself into one rigid style, remember the first rule of thumb about decorating: Please yourself. While you may want to emulate a certain look, don't become a slave to it and squash your creative spirit along the way. The key is to build a room around a theme or a mood while carefully incorporating your personality into it. A favorite color is one good way to do this, or a repeated motif or pattern.

When considering style, everyone needs a little inspiration. Think about rooms you have admired and what attracted you. Was it a painted finish? A pretty fabric? Beautiful window treatments? Elegant cabinetry? Artful accessories? How did the room make you feel? Cheerful? Nostalgic? Restful? Energetic?

You can also take a clue from the rest of your home. Look at the style of the architecture. Is it contemporary? Colonial? Are there elaborate trims and moldings, or are the walls, doors, and windows streamlined and spare? Even if the architecture is nondescript, you can introduce a period flavor with reproduction fixtures, window treatments, wall-coverings, and accessories. Is there a theme you have already established with the rest of your furnishings and decoration? Do you like antiques? Are you a collector or someone who prefers a pared-down look? You can build on these features and preferences in the new bathroom or depart from them entirely if you wish. Find one transitional element, such as the floor treatment or the color scheme, to create a visual bridge so the change from room to room isn't abrupt.

Whatever you do, your approach to decorating the new bath should be deliberate. Let it evolve over time. Don't rush your choices. Live with paint and wallpaper samples for a while.

Above: *Curls and swirls at the vanity area offset the long, rectilinear shape of the room.*
Opposite: *A playful juxtaposition of the right angles and curves is all the decoration this bath needs. Boxy little towel nooks echo the marble tile squares.*

To help you discover what look is right for you, this chapter offers a brief description of popular decorating styles. Feel free to follow them or design a variation on one of these themes. Remember, colors, patterns, and other materials are suggestions. Use them as starting points, but let your own preferences guide you in the end.

TRADITIONAL

Today's traditional style incorporates elements of English and American eighteenth- and early nineteenth-century design. The look is rich and formal. Select wood cabinetry, finished in a mellow wood stain or painted white, with details like fluted panels, bulls-eye corner blocks, and dentil and crown molding. The cabinet's door style is usually a raised panel, sometimes slightly arched. Fabricate an elegant countertop with marble—or a plastic laminate that's a faux version. Hand-painted tiles work well, too. Hardware and fittings in polished brass will add a sophisticated Old World touch. Colors may include Wedgwood blue or deeply hued jewel tones. Patterns based on nature-inspired themes, such as flowers or birds, as well as formal stripes and tapestry or crewel work look-alikes work well in traditional rooms. You might want to include an antique wardrobe in this bathroom for heirloom linens

or nestle a Windsor chair next to the bath. Strictly speaking, success with traditional style lies in managing the details. Visit an architectural salvage shop to replace contemporary fixtures with gilded mirrors, wall sconces, and high-arched faucets, or shop for faithful reproductions. Install divided-light windows and dress them with a formal window treatment, such as swags paired with drapery panels and sheers. For added privacy, use shutters or wood blinds along with your curtains.

Traditional Smart Tip Retrofit an antique chest for bathroom storage, but make sure you properly seal the wood against moisture. If you really want to be smart, buy a new cabinet that's made to look like an antique and won't fall prey to the assaults of humidity and water. Your old chest left open to display linens, soaps, and pretty bottled toiletries will create a focal point for the room.

Opposite: *This design successfully bridges contemporary architecture with updated traditional details.*
Left: *An heirloom chest and chair complement Traditional décor.*

COUNTRY

Call it pure Americana, English, Swedish, Italian, or French. The style is basic, casual, and warm—and every country has its own version. "Country" often implies a deeper connection with the outdoors and the simple life than other styles and uses an abundance of natural elements. Start with plain wood cabinetry stained a light maple, or add a distressed, crackled, or pickled finish. Door styles are usually framed, sometimes with a raised panel. Install a laminate countertop, and coordinate it with the tile you select for the room. Hand-painted tiles with a simple theme lend a custom touch.

For added country charm, stencil a wall border or select a wallpaper pattern with a folk-art motif or floral prints. Checks and ticking stripes are also popular in a country-style room—on the wall, as a tile pattern, or on the shower-curtain fabric. If you feel creative, apply a painted finish to the wall. Otherwise, check out the many wallpaper designs on the market that emulate the look of sponging, ragging, combing, and other special painted effects.

Install a double-hung window in the room. (Casement windows look too contemporary in this setting.) Some window treatment ideas include a balloon topper over mini blinds or shutters, for privacy, combined with a matching or contrasting lace café curtain. If you have a casement window in the bathroom that you do not want to change, install pop-in muntins to give the unit more of a traditional or old-fashioned look.

Above: *Pine cabinetry and earthy floor titles combine with an elegant floral print wallcovering to make this country bath both rustic and refined.*
Opposite: *A meadow green paint color, picked up from the wallpaper print, puts a fresh face on shutters and wainscoting*

A skirted pedestal sink or pine chest-turned-vanity, along with reproduction faucets, will add a nostalgic charm to a country bathroom. Bring a playful note to this informal design with whimsical hardware fabricated in wrought iron, brushed pewter, or porcelain. Hardware and fittings that are polished look too refined for this style.

Popular country colors include red gingham and denim blue. Choose a checkerboard floor or a mosaic of broken tiles if hardwood is not available. Or consider laminate flooring that gives you the look of real wood without the mainte-

nance. Some styles even come with a painted-floor design. The country bath is the type of room that begs for baskets, old bottles, and ceramic vases filled with wildflowers. Accessorize with these items or a collection of favorite things, and you've created a very personal space.

Country Smart Tip Collections are often part of a country décor, even in the bathroom. All you need is three or more of anything that have size, shape, or color in common. You can mass them on walls, on shelves, on the windowsills, or even along the edge of the tub.

SHAKER

The basic tenants of the Shaker philosophy, which evolved out of a nineteenth-century religious movement, are built on a sense of humbleness. This is reflected in the way Shakers designed their furniture and homes. They believed in using only the most essential elements, completely without ornamentation or frills. Their plain, practical, home-spun designs featured dovetailed joints and hand-planed tops, plain panels on doors, and legs tapered almost to a pencil point. Finishes were always dyes or oils, never varnishes, to enhance the wood.

Contemporary cabinet manufacturers, responding to a renewed popularity of the Shaker look over the last decade, have used the Shakers original designs to inspire similar updated versions of their own. When shopping for Shaker-style cabinetry for your new bath, look for the same plain paneled doors and wood finishes that are engineered to hold up against moisture. You can hang a matching medicine cabinet or install a mirror with a plain wood frame over the sink. A typically Shaker slanted rack of shelves that can be freestanding or mounted to the wall works well in the room, acting as extra storage for towels and soaps. Place several of the round wooden Shaker stacking boxes on the shelves. You can find them unfinished in craft stores. Lightly sand them, and then apply paint in a color picked up from the woodwork.

Keeping simplicity in mind, paint the walls in your Shaker-inspired bath white or cream. Accent woodwork with a muted shade of slate blue, brick red, or harvest gold. Install plain fixtures in white or cream tones with unfussy fittings. Ceramic tile arranged in a quiltlike pattern can add more color accents and a reasonable amount of decoration, unless you're a purist at heart.

A traditional double-hung window, with or without muntins, fits in fine with the Shaker theme. For privacy, hang plain wood shutters and panel-style curtains with tab tops that have been fabricated in simple cotton or muslin. A tin chandelier paired with tin wall sconces will pull the look together.

If there's room, place a Shaker-style ladder-back chair with a woven-tape seat in a corner of the room, and hang an old embroidered print on the wall.

Shaker Smart Tip This warm, likable style fits in perfectly with a country home because of its old-fashioned values. But it blends in well with contemporary interiors, too, because of its clean lines and plain geometric shapes. In fact, adding a few Shaker elements can warm up the sometimes cold look of a thoroughly modern room.

Above: *Contemporary style glorifies unaccessorized architectural forms. This undulating glass-block shower wall has a visual effect as well as a practical function.*
Opposite: *This simple solution to storage epitomizes the practical philosophy behind Shaker style.*

CONTEMPORARY

What we refer to as "contemporary style" evokes images of clean architectural lines, an absence of decoration and color, and materials like chrome, glass, and stone. Indeed, its roots are at the turn of the last century, when architects and designers flatly rejected the exaggerated artificial

Right: *A whimsical wallcovering of decoupaged newspaper clippings and random squares of color put an individualistic face on this modern eclectic-style bath. The decoesque vanity and mirror resemble an early twentieth-century dressing table.*

embellishments of the Victorians by turning to natural products and pared-down forms. Various modern movements, evolving over the course of the twentieth century, gradually incorporated new manmade materials into their streamlined forms. Hence the high-tech look popularized in the 1970s and 1980s.

Today, contemporary style is taking a softer turn, even in the bathroom, a place where hard edges, cool reflective surfaces, and cutting-edge technology abound. Bath designers are taking another look at time-honored forms and giving them a new spin. It's not unusual to see updated versions of traditional fixtures and fittings, for example, or new uses for natural materials in a contemporary bathroom. This is especially true as improved finishes have made these products more durable and easier to maintain. And although black and white are classic mainstays in any style, the stark-white palette identified with contemporary design over the last two decades has been replaced with earthy hues or warmer shades of white.

When selecting cabinets for your contemporary bath, pair a frameless door with a wood finish. Laminate cabinetry is still compatible with this style, but for an updated look, wood is it. For interest, don't be afraid to mix several materials and finishes on cabinets and other surfaces throughout the room. Combinations of wood and various metals, such as chrome, copper, brass, and pewter, make strong statements, as does the duo of stone and glass. Used on countertops or to fabricate the sink, shower, or tub surrounds, mixed materials keep the room from looking sterile. For more visual interest apply a glazed or textured finish to neutral-colored walls. And bring as much of the outdoors into this room as possible. Install casement-style windows and skylights or roof windows to blend with con-

temporary architecture. For privacy, use tailored Roman shades or vertical blinds on the windows.

Contemporary Smart Tip Incorporate elements of Arts and Crafts, Art Deco, or other designs associated with the modern movement of the twentieth century (International Style, Bauhaus, Memphis, and the influence of Scandinavian design). Their clean geometric lines are quite compatible with this environment. This eclectic approach can be very sophisticated. Look for framed art prints, a vintage-inspired wallpaper, or reproduction hardware, faucets, or light fixtures to underscore your theme. Fortunately, manufacturers are reproducing art tiles from original molds or designs that can be used as accents.

NEOCLASSICAL

Neoclassical mimics the style of ancient Roman and Greek design. It developed in the late-eighteenth to mid-nineteenth centuries upon the excavation of the ruins of Pompeii and influenced furniture design of that era, including Federal and Empire styles. It is enjoying renewed popularity. Today's version incorporates classic architectural and design themes, including columns, pediments, ornate carvings and plasterwork, curvaceous shapes, and decorating motifs, such as urns, scrolls, and shield shapes. It is highly ornamental.

To achieve this opulent look, select formal-style wood cabinetry with heavy carving and ornate molding. Lavish the scheme with rich materials, such as a marble tub fabricated

Below: *The lavish size of this master bath would satisfy a Roman emperor. To add even more drama to its opulent looks, the designer specified a marbled finish on all the woodwork and cabinetry.*

in one of a variety of white and pastel shades. Build the tub into a platform set off by columns. If solid marble or tiles are beyond your budget, opt for a look-alike in solid-surfacing material that can be used to form the tub, shower, sink, countertops, and even the bathroom floor.

Don't skimp on the details—this bath truly defines luxury. Go ahead and pamper yourself with gold-plated fittings and a chandelier. Install gilded sconces on either side of the vanity and use accent lighting strips to draw attention to handsome details, such as crown molding.

Colors that enhance the neoclassical look include white, off-white, black, gray, or gold, as well as earth tones, such as sepia. Today, special painted effects and wallpaper that mimic stone (a throwback to those ancient stone villas) or soft, buttery leather pull everything together. Top it off with a wallpaper border or stencil that features an architectural motif or one that resembles swagged fabric.

An arched-top window suits a neoclassical bathroom perfectly. Dress it with a swag window treatment. For privacy, add either a Roman or pleated shade.

Neoclassical Smart Tip

Instead of expensive hand-crafted plasterwork, look into the many pre-fabricated moldings, ceiling medallions, pillars, cornices, and the like that are made of lightweight molded plastic. They can be faux painted to resemble marble or stone and are fairly easy to install yourself.

that combines light, airy colors with pretty, feminine curlicues, cutouts, and curves.

Black and white tiles set in a diamond pattern will fit right in here, as will wainscoting or molding painted a crisp white to match porcelain pieces. For lighting, include wall sconces and ceiling fixtures that mimic old gas lamps. A weathered wood floor will make this room cozy, too, especially topped with a charming hand-hooked rug.

On the wall, decorate with pretty wallpaper that features a floral motif or a complex paisley—two designs popular during the Victorian era. For an authentic look, mix more than one pattern. Don't be afraid of creating a mismatched mess. The trick to doing this successfully is sticking to the same colors—no matter how many different patterns you add to your decorating scheme.

For window treatments, select lace, such as a delicate Battenburg design. Carry this theme over to your shower curtain, too. For privacy, install a lace pleated shade or a ballon shade.

A small bamboo table or a white wicker piece always adds charm to room like this. If there's enough space, bring in a wicker vanity, shelves, or a small chair.

VICTORIAN

Anyone who likes nostalgia will appreciate this romantic, highly ornamented look. Think gingerbread, think lace. Use traditional-style, raised-panel doors painted white. Select cabinetry that features lots of decorative millwork, such as cutout panels. A graceful pedestal sink with a high-arc brass faucet or a lav with a pretty skirted bottom would be suitable in a Victorian setting. Choose antique fixtures and fittings in brass or a mixture of brass and porcelain, or shop for reproduction models. Well-known manufacturers offer a line of claw-footed tubs, pedestals, high-tank toilets, and the like to suit this décor. Some Victorian looks are very formal, with heavy patterns and lots of deep colors. Others are more casual and have a Victorian country-style appeal

Victorian Smart Tip Victorian, today, is a very romantic look. To underscore this, add the scent of lavender or some other dried flower to the room or use potpourri, which you can keep in a bowl on the vanity. Hang a fragrant pomander on a hook, display lavender soaps on a wall shelf, or tuck sachets between towels on a shelf. For an authentic touch, display a Victorian favorite, the spider plant.

ARTS & CRAFTS

The Arts and Crafts Movement, with roots at the turn of the twentieth century, was a reaction to the ornamentation of Victorian design and the growing use of machines to produce cheap goods. It also professed a philosophy that beautiful, simple, organic objects arranged harmoniously in a house will contribute to one's well-being. The movement's aesthetic is enjoying a resurgence today. Styles that are related to or part of the Arts and Crafts Movement include Mission, Craftsman, and Prairie (Frank Lloyd Wright's signature style).

Start with plain oak cabinets with a hand-crafted appearance. As with Shaker style, manufacturers are responding to the public interest in Arts and Crafts style today, and some offer a line of authentically inspired cabinets. Accessorize with hand-hammered copper hardware. If you can't find genuine examples, shop for reproductions.

The more wood the better in an Arts and Crafts-style room. Oil the wood well to bring out the grain, and properly seal it against water damage.

For the walls, combine an oak wainscot with a stylized wallpaper—one that combines floral motifs within a geometric pattern. There are wallpaper manufacturers who specialize in this style. Select colors that reflect the hues of nature, such as brown, green, blue, and orange. Accessorize with organically shaped pottery in these colors. Pull it together by incorporating native American textiles into this motif, too.

For tile, select natural colors and textures or ones with matte or "art pottery" glazes, such as crys-

Opposite: *True to an Arts and Crafts aesthetic, the handsome oak cabinetry and woodwork take center stage. Art-glass sconces are reproductions.*
Right: *The muted color of the walls and unobtrusive quality of the all-glass shower underscore the simplicity of the design.*

talline. Lighting fixtures can include a combination of unobtrusive recessed canisters and wall fixtures with Tiffany-style glass covers or mica shades. You may want to include a Mission-style chair or small table in the room.

Plain windows should be curtained very simply in an Arts and Crafts-style room, using natural fabrics, such as linen or muslin, with an embroidered border. Typical motifs include ginkgo leaves and poppy seeds. Preferably, instead of traditional treatments, use stained glass or art glass windows, which will provide privacy and a dramatic play of light. There are several manufacturers today that are producing an Arts and Crafts line of stained-glass windows.

Arts and Crafts Smart Tip The heart of this style rests in its earthy connection. The more you can bring nature into it, the more authentic it will be. An easy way to do this is with plants. A bonus is that plants naturally thrive in the bathroom where they enjoy the humid environment.

ART DECO

Dramatic and a bit exotic, Art Deco is the forerunner of modern design. It evolved during the first two decades of the twentieth century. Hallmarks include a flamboyant use of geometric shapes, pastel colors, and lots of chrome.

In today's Art Deco-influenced bathroom, start with contemporary cabinetry. A vanity with a rounded or tubular-shape front and frameless doors is perfect. For countertop material, check out stainless steel, chrome, or glass, or install a solid-surfacing material with a bullnose edge. Hang a round frameless mirror above the sink. Streamlined fixtures and reproduction chrome faucets from the 1920s and 1930s will look great in an Art Deco-style bath. Accent with color, especially in tiles designed in a geometric pattern, such as a zigzag or a sunburst. Black and white are the basic tones to begin with; then add blasts of bright pastels, such as pinks, corals, and turquoise.

This is a look that can be serious or playful. For inspiration, look at pictures of early twentieth-century Miami architecture, much of which still exists, or the great ocean liners of pre World War II.

Like contemporary baths, Art Deco-style rooms call for simple windows with spare treatments. Install blinds for a paired-down modern look.

Art Deco Smart Tip One thing you don't want in an Art Deco room is ornament. You can mix elements of contemporary style with this look, however. To give this room interest, rely on lots of sleek shiny surfaces. Apply a lacquered finish to cabinetry. Display prints in glossy lacquered frames painted in bright pastel colors. Use chrome accessories, such as soap dishes, vases, and towel bars.

THE DECORATING PHASE

Once you've determined the style that suits your personality, you can begin to take the steps that will pull together the entire project. Remember, using a particular style as a guide is helpful, but listen to your own instincts when decorating. Begin the decorating phase of your bath project by following these simple steps:

SMART STEPS

ONE: *Create a Sample Board.* Don't make your bathroom decorating all trial and error. Try out your ideas on a sample board first. To make one, use a piece of $1/2$-inch plywood, which is heavy enough to hold your samples but light enough for you to handle. Mount your samples—paint chips, fabric swatches, flooring and tile samples, countertop chips, and any other material you plan to bring into the room—on the board to see how each one works as part of an overall scheme. The larger the sample, the better. If a wallpaper pattern clashes with the color or pattern of the tile, change one or both until you find a match. The board lets you test ideas before you start buying materials and make costly mistakes.

Try different combinations of colors and patterns. Look at them under all types of light, night and day. Add photographs of fixtures or materials you may want to include in the room but don't have samples of to put on the board.

Create a cheat sheet, based on your sample boards, to take with you when shopping. Your sample board is a wonderful resource for building a room that works together in harmony. (Note: Remembering color shade accurately is nearly impossible. Working without a guide is a sure way to end up with something that doesn't match.)

When creating your sample board, include your sources. Note store names for every item, as well as manufacturers. If there are model numbers and color names, write them down, too. This will be invaluable if you ever have to do a touchup or replace an item in the room later. Your sample board also may come in handy if you decide to redecorate adjoining rooms. With all your samples, it won't be so difficult to achieve a cohesive or compatible style.

Right: *Eastern influences on contemporary Western design can be seen in the simplicity of form and content in this space.*

Opposite: *A mirrored recess next to the tub reflects some of the garden into the bath.*
Right: *The view of the tub, as seen in the mirrored doors, creates an attractive sight line near the vanity.*

TWO: *Note the Sight Lines.* A sight line is the visual path the eye follows from a given point within a room or from an entrance. A room's primary sight line is at the entry. It is the most important one because it draws your attention into the room. Your eye immediately moves in one direction toward whatever is directly opposite the doorway. Very often in a bathroom that focus will be the tub, but it could be the toilet. Hopefully, it's not. The time for relocating fixtures is not at the deco-rating stage. However, if you're still in the planning process and reading this chapter for ideas, you should review the fixture place-ments in your base map and look over Chapter Two, "Function—Up Close and Personal."

Once you're inside a room, there are other sight lines to consider. In today's spalike bathing environments, they have become more significant because people spend more time in the bathroom, whether to read, relax, exercise, or even socialize. Begin noting sight lines at the tub area. What will you face when you're sitting in it? Who wouldn't enjoy a bubble bath next to a pretty view to the outdoors? If that's not a possibility, looking at attractive wall art is better than staring at the toilet.

Move to other places in the bathroom where you are apt to linger. Examine all of the sight lines reflected in any mir-rors, not just the one over the vanity. Contemporary bath-rooms, particularly spacious master baths, can contain a lot of mirrored and glass surfaces that draw attention to things that might otherwise go unnoticed, such as piping under a pedestal sink, the toilet area, or dead corners. Think about how you want to move your eye around the room, too. Sight lines should be fluid. You don't want your eye to jump from one element to the next. You want it to move from the curve of the sink up to the roundness of the mir-ror, for example. Use repeated color and pattern to create a rhythm that will carry your vision from one place to the next. If there are a lot boxy corners that stop the flow, introduce a few curved or rounded shapes around the room. When you want to draw attention to something, highlight it with a color that contrasts with the rest of the room or accent it with light. On the other hand, you can play down an unattractive feature or sight line using the same devices for diverting the eye elsewhere.

Sight lines in the home are the same as lines in a painting or in a graphic design. What pulls the eye should be continuous. Find balance and symmetry in your sight lines. Don't place all of the most powerful visual elements on one side of the room. Plan some way to attract attention to the farthest corners and the most uninspired sections of the room. It could be the addition of a single accessory that does the trick. Fill a basket with colorful towels or soaps, or artfully arrange a collection of *anything* on a wall.

THREE: *Add Details.* More than anything else, it is the details in a room that people react to and remember—the Shaker pegged towel rack or the curlicued wicker chair. Details have a powerful effect on the feeling or mood of the room, too. They usually make the difference between a room that looks professionally designed and one that lacks polish. With details, you are bringing personality and something of yourself into the space.

Some of the best details you can include are the smallest—drawer pulls you picked up at an antique store, an old mantle you found at an architectural salvage yard that makes the perfect shelf above the toilet in the powder room, pretty shells in a glass jar or just left on the countertop.

No matter how big or small the room, details will pull the style together. Add period flavor with crown molding. Dress up contemporary fixtures with polished stone fittings. Display items you like in artful ways on the walls, shelves, or countertop. Don't worry if it's a collection of disparate objects, sizes, and shapes. Anything connected by a theme will work. Different prints in the same frame or with the same matting will do. Mix photographs with paintings or other odd objects. Group things for impact, such as a collection of candles near the tub for a candlelit soak. Display your favorite holiday momentos, kids art, or odd pieces of old china in the room.

When arranging, keep scale and proportion in mind. A large object on a small surface looks awkward; a small object on large surface looks odd, too. When grouping things, balance one large object with several small ones. Practice your arrangements on the floor before hanging them, or sketch them to scale on paper first.

Left: *A lined wicker basket next to a tub makes a charming receptacle for linens.* **Opposite:** *The lattice tub surround is the detail that pulls together a Victorian garden theme.*

Right: *A cheerful shade of yellow brightens the boxed-in area around the tub. The neutral background on the tiles tones down the intensity of this color.*
Opposite: *Wood details, such as the trim, the shoji screen, and the strips of wood inlaid into the stone floor, underpin the Japanese-inspired theme in this bathroom.*

If you still want to stick with white or beige for the tub, sink, and toilet, introduce color to the walls or with accessories. Just pick up a can of paint and see how color can transform the space in no time at all. If you don't like what you've done, just grab another can of paint and start again. It's inexpensive and easy to apply.

One of the simplest things you can do to test out a color is to apply it to a sheet of white poster board, hang it on the wall, and live with it a few days. Look at it during the day; then wait for evening and look at it again under varying levels of artificial light. Is the color still appealing to you? What effect does it have on the space at different times of the day? Even if you're thinking about tiling a wall or installing wallpaper, pick out the dominant color, find a matching paint, and apply this simple test.

FOUR: *Use Color.* Color is probably your greatest decorating tool. Don't be afraid of it—it also happens to be one of the easiest things to change. So why do people typically stick with a neutral palette in the bathroom? A dated color on a permanent fixture can be expensive to replace if you're replacing the entire fixture. However, new paints make it possible to refurbish ceramic and porcelain with new color for a fraction of the cost of replacement.

Color has amazing properties. It can evoke memories, create a mood, or even change your perception of space. Light colors expand a room, darker colors draw the walls inward. This is also true of ceilings. If you have a high ceiling that seems out of proportion to the small measurements of the room, you may want to paint it a dark color for contrast and to force the perspective in the room. What you are doing is creating an optical illusion.

Opposite: *Cool gray slate on the walls and floor balances the hot reds and yellow in this bathroom.*
Left: *The green and lavender-pink tiles play up Art Nouveau style, a decorative movement of the late nineteenth and early twentieth centuries.*

As a rule of thumb, use no more than three colors in one room. There really can be too much of a good thing. Use the colors in unique amounts and, perhaps, in different shades and tints. A monochromatic (one color) scheme will produce a calming effect. Unfortunately, it can also appear dull and uninspired. You can counteract the monotony of one color by using it in various shades, textures, and patterns. One easy way to accomplish this is with a painted finish like ragging, sponging, or glazing.

The stronger a color, the less of it is used. That's another general rule, which can be broken by your personal preference, of course. A dollop of saturated red equals an entire wall of pale pink in visual weight.

When you use two or three colors, combine unequal amounts and different shades of each one along with a

dash of black, white, or another neutral. If you don't, your eyes won't know where to focus. Let one color dominate. Anchor your accent colors in opposite parts of the room. For example, you can pick up a color from the wallpaper in the towels hanging by the tub, and then use the same color in a vase on the vanity countertop.

Where do you get your color inspiration? Forget about color fads. Look at the world around you. For an explosion of color, visit the produce aisle of the grocery store. Comb through fashion magazines and art books. Look at your own closet! Tear out pictures of anything with color that attracts and pleases you. Keep a record in your design notebook. After you've got a stack of these tear sheets, divide them up by color. Undoubtedly a pattern will emerge. Whatever color dominates that collection is a good indicator of what pleases you most of the time.

WALLPAPER, PAINT, AND FABRIC IN THE BATHROOM

While you're thinking about color for the new bathroom, consider the type of paint, wallpaper, and fabric to use. Remember, bathrooms have lots of glossy surfaces, which reflect light. Unless you want an intense effect, opt for low-luster paints and matte finishes. If you are concerned about moisture, especially in a room without a duct vent, shop for products that have been treated with mildewcide in the manufacturing process. Moist areas are perfect breeding grounds for mold. When moisture seeps behind wallpaper, it creates a moldy, peeling mess. Luckily, this is a problem that can be avoided because you'll find there is a wide available selection of products and glues that are designed specifically for bathroom applications.

After you've settled on a color scheme, you can look for wallpaper and fabrics to carry your theme through. Use them, later, to pick up a solid color for accents or trim. Two major factors in deciding the patterns to choose are the location and size of the room. Review the sight lines from outside the bathroom. Look at the adjoining areas, especially the ones that you must pass through to get to the bathroom. Think of them sequentially. Ideally, you should create an interrelationship between all the patterns and colors that run from room to room. If you want stripes in the bath but the adjoining hallway has a floral wallpaper, match the colors. In a small bathroom, as a rule, a bold print may be too busy. On the other hand, it may be just what is needed to make a large space feel cozier. Vertical designs will add height to a room. Conversely, horizontal motifs will draw the eye around it. In general, patterned wallpaper looks best in a traditional-style room. In a contemporary setting, subtle patterns that don't detract from the architecture and the materials are best. And always avoid trendy looks, unless you want to make changes every couple of years.

Lastly, texture is a way to bring visual interest to the bathroom. Some paints and papers come with a textured finish, or you can create your own illusion of one with special techniques, such as sponging, ragging, graining, and combing. Simple do-it-yourself kits are inexpensive and available at home centers, hardware stores, and craft shops. If you're not in the painting mood, there are wallpaper patterns that are printed to look like these effects.

Left: *The striped wallpaper adds a tailored appearance to this room, but the coordinating floral fabric on the curtains keeps this design from looking too formal.*
Opposite: *Cotton and linen fabrics that can be dry cleaned or washed are good choices for a bathroom.*

REMODELING TIMELINE AT A GLANCE

There are many variables that can affect the pace and timing of your bathroom remodeling project. Every contractor works differently, and each job may present its own small—or large—glitches. However, there are steps that divide up the process into logical sequences that eventually result in a finished bathroom.

Here's a timeline of events that will help you to gauge—in a sequential fashion—the work that is involved. The estimated time lengths indicated here for the various stages are for an average-sized bathroom using standard products and materials. Keep in mind that the time indicated is approximate. Depending on the scope of your project, it may be shorter or longer. For example, any custom items (cabinets, faucets, colored fixtures) require an 8- to-12-week lead time that will hold up the work accordingly.

SMART STEPS

ONE *Preplanning*
- Make the decision to remodel
- Assess the problems and goals involved
- Gather ideas and review trends
- Develop a budget and obtain financing
- Collect information about contractors
- Arrange interview with contractor

THREE *Design & Agreement*
- Presentation of preliminary drawings and project specifications
- Review and discuss options
- Sign a design agreement

| 4 weeks | 1 week | 2–3 weeks | 2–4 weeks |

TWO *Initial Meetings*
- Walk-through of the existing space
- Brainstorm with the contractor
- Decide whether project is feasible within the budget
- Sign a letter of intent if purchasing design services, or skip to step 4

FOUR *Design Development/Preconstruction*
- Review completed drawings and project notes
- Clarify any misunderstandings about the scope and intent of the project
- Select products
- Sign the construction contract
- Make first downpayment
- Wait three days for the Right of Recision period to pass, if applicable
- Obtain permits
- Meet with construction team and sign preconstruction agreement

FIVE *After Permits Are Issued*

- ❦ Order products
- ❦ Finalize project schedule and distribute
- ❦ Discuss impact of project on home life with family, including safety and keeping pets out of the workplace
- ❦ Remove personal items and breakables from construction area

SEVEN *The Final Stages*

- ❦ Inspect the job, and establish list of final details to make sure everything is completed to your satisfaction
- ❦ Obtain final inspection and certificate of occupancy or habitability
- ❦ Make substantial completion payment

1 week	4–8 weeks	1 week	1 week

SIX *The Work*

- ❦ Complete demolition
- ❦ Complete framing
- ❦ Rough-in mechanical systems
- ❦ Install drywall
- ❦ Install flooring
- ❦ Install cabinetry
- ❦ Install fixtures
- ❦ Do finishing work (painting and wallpapering)

EIGHT *The Conclusion*

- ❦ Give final approval
- ❦ Make final payment

CONCLUSION

Designing and remodeling a bath is not easy. It requires attention to detail, organization, and endless planning. It may also require a good deal of temporary inconvenience—especially if the bathroom is the only one in the house. But, it is also incredibly rewarding. Education is your most powerful tool. Learn all you can about design. And, just keep smiling—through the dust, the inconvenience, and the intrusion of workmen traipsing in and out of your home. Believe it or not, order will be restored eventually, and you'll have a beautiful new bathroom that will not only make your life better, but will add to the overall value of your house.

As you go along, don't be afraid to try new things on paper. But don't get in over your head. Ask for help when you need it. Professional assistance can be the difference between disaster and perfection.

When things get a little crazy—and they will—keep your eye on the goal and imagine your first zesty shower or soothing soak in the new space. Through it all, you're bound to get a bit impatient with the process. You may even wonder why you started it at all! But once the taps are running, and the wallpaper is hung, you'll be so glad you did. 🐚

Left: *An expansive mirror above the vanity, glass-door cabinets, and a large window make this bathroom seem bigger. The pale color scheme creates a soothing effect.*

Appendix: Basic Bathroom Planning Guidelines

According to the National Kitchen & Bath Association, there are over 40 million pre-existing houses in the United States. Very often, these homes contain a typical-sized 5 x 7-foot bathroom. That doesn't leave much space for more than a standard tub, toilet, and lavatory, so professional designers encourage remodelers to expand these small baths to accommodate more amenities and to provide greater space for maneuvering safely and comfortably. The NKBA has developed a comprehensive list of bathroom planning guidelines that help both bath design professionals and homeowners who are designing a bath remodel on their own—whether or not expansion is an option. These guidelines appear here with the expressed permission of the NKBA.

1a. Doorways at least 32 inches wide and not more than 24 inches deep in the direction of travel.

1b. The clear space at a doorway must be measured at the narrowest point.

1c. Walkways should be a minimum of 36 inches wide.

2. Clear floor space at least the width of the door on the push side and a larger clear floor space on the pull side for maneuvering to open, close, and pass through the doorway.

3. A minimum clear floor space of 30 x 48 inches either parallel or perpendicular should be provided at the lavatory.

4a. A minimum clear floor space of 48 x 48 inches provided in front of the toilet with 16 inches of that clear floor space extending to each side of the fixture's centerline.

4b. Up to 12 inches of the 48 x 48 inches of clear floor space can extend under the lavatory when total access to a knee space is provided.

5. A minimum clear floor space of 48 x 48 inches from the front of the bidet should be provided.

6a. A minimum clear floor space of 60 x 30 inches at the bathtub for a parallel approach.

6b. A minimum clear floor space of 60 x 48 inches at the bathtub for a perpendicular approach.

7. A minimum clear floor space at a shower less than 60 inches wide should be 36 inches deep x shower width + 12 inches. A shower 60 inches wide or greater requires a space of 36 inches deep x shower width.

8. The clear floor spaces required at each fixture may overlap.

9. Turning space of 180 degrees planned for in the bathroom. Minimum diameter of 60 inches for 360-degree turns and/or T-turn with a space of 36 x 36 x 60 inches.

10. A minimum clear floor space of 30 x 48 inches is required beyond the door swing in the bathroom.

11. For more than one vanity, one may be 30–34 inches and another 34–42 inches high.

12. Kneespace provided at the lavatory, 27 inches above the floor at the front edge and 30 inches wide.

13. The bottom edge of the mirror over the lavatory should be a maximum of 40 inches above the floor or a maximum of 48 inches above the floor if it is tilted.

14. The minimum clear floor space from the centerline of the lavatory to any side wall is 15 inches.

15. The minimum clearance between two bowls in the lavatory center is 30 inches, centerline to centerline.

16. In an enclosed shower, the minimum usable interior dimensions are 34 x 34 inches measured wall to wall.

17. Showers should include a bench or seat that is 17–19 inches above the floor and a minimum of 15 inches deep.

18. A 60-inch shower requires a 32-inch entrance. If the shower is 42 inches deep, 36 inches is required.

19. Shower doors must open into the bathroom.

20. No steps at the tub or shower area. Safety rails should be installed to facilitate transfer.

21. All showerheads equipped with a pressure-balance/temperance regulator or temperature-limiting device.

22a. Shower controls accessible from inside and outside the fixture and located between 38–48 inches above the floor and offset toward the room.

22b. Tub controls accessible from inside and outside the fixture and located between the tub rim and 33 inches above the floor, below the grab bar and offset toward room.

23a. A minimum 16-inch clearance from the centerline of the toilet or bidet to any obstruction on either side.

23b. For adjacent toilet and bidet installation, the 16-inch minimum clearance to all obstructions should be maintained.

24. The toilet-paper holder installed within reach of person seated on the toilet, slightly in front of the edge of the toilet and centered 26 inches above the floor.

25. Compartmentalized toilet areas should be a minimum of 36 x 66 inches with a swing-out door or pocket door.

26. Walls reinforced to receive grab bars in the tub, shower, and toilet areas.

27. Storage for toiletries, linens, grooming, and general bathroom supplies provided 15–48 inches above the floor.

28. Storage for soap, towels, and personal hygiene items should be installed within reach of person seated on bidet or toilet or within 15–48 inches above the floor and do not interfere with use of fixture.

29. In the tub/shower area, storage for soap and personal hygiene items provided with 15–48 inches above the floor.

30. All flooring should be slip-resistant.

31. Exposed pipes and mechanicals covered by protective panel or shroud.

32. Controls, dispensers, outlets, and operating mechanisms 15–48 inches above the floor and operable with a closed fist.

33. Access panel to all mechanical, electrical, and plumbing systems.

34. Mechanical ventilation systems included to vent entire room. Calculation for minimum size of system: Cubic space (LxWxH) x 8 (changes per hour) = minimum cubic feet per minute (CFM) 60 minutes

35. Ground fault circuit interrupters specified on all receptacles, lights, and switches. All light fixtures above the tub/shower must be moisture-proof, special-purpose fixtures.

36. Auxiliary heating may be planned in an addition to the primary heat source.

37. Every function should be well illuminated with task lighting, night lights, and/or general lighting. No lighting fixtures should be within reach of person seated or standing in tub or shower.

38. Bathroom lighting should include a window/skylight area equal to a minimum of 10 percent of bathroom's square footage.

39. Controls, handles, and door/drawer pulls should be operable with one hand, require minimal strength, and do not require tight grasp, pinching, or twisting of wrist.

40. Use clipped or radius corners for open countertops and eased to eliminate sharp edges.

41. Any glass in a tub/shower partition or other glass application within 18 inches of the floor should be laminated glass with a plastic interlayer, tempered glass, or approved plastic.

GLOSSARY

OF BATH TERMS

Absorption (light): All substances absorb light at different wavelengths. The color depends on the wavelength reflected.

Accent Lighting: A type of lighting that highlights an area or object to emphasize that aspect of a room's character.

Accessible: Refers to design that accommodates persons with physical disabilities.

Accessories: Towel racks, soap dishes, and other items specifically designed for use in the bath. ▼

Adaptable: Refers to design that can be easily changed to accommodate a person with disabilities.

Ambient Light: General illumination that surrounds a room. There is no visible source of the light.

Antiscalding Valve (Pressure-Balancing Valve): A single-control fitting that contains a piston that automatically responds to changes in line water pressure to maintain temperature; the value blocks abrupt drop or rise in temperature.

Apron: The front extension of a bathtub that runs from the rim to floor.

Awning Window: A window with a single framed-glass panel. It is hinged at the top to swing out when it is open.

Backlighting: Illumination coming from a source behind or at the side of an object.

Barrier-Free Fixtures: Fixtures specifically designed for people who use wheelchairs or who have limited mobility.

Basin: A shallow sink.

Base Cabinet: A cabinet that rests on the floor under a countertop or vanity.

Base Plan: A map of an existing bathroom that shows detailed measurements and location of fixtures and their permanent elements.

Bidet: A bowl-shaped fixture that supplies water for personal hygiene. It looks similar to a toilet.

Built-In: A cabinet, shelf, medicine chest, or other storage unit that is recessed into the wall. ▲

Bump Out: Living space created by cantilevering the floor and ceiling joists and extending the exterior wall of a room.

Candlepower (Cp): The intensity of light measured at the light source.

Cantilever: A structural beam supported on one end. A cantilever can be used to support a small addition.

Casement Window: A window that consists of one framed-glass panel and is hinged on the side. It swings outward from the opening at the turn of a crank.

Centerline: The dissecting line through the center of an object, such as a sink.

CFM: An abbreviation that refers to cubic feet of air that is moved per minute by an exhaust fan.

Clearance: The amount of space between two fixtures, the centerlines of two fixtures, or a fixture and an obstacle, such as a wall. Clearances may be mandated by codes.

Code: A locally and/or nationally enforced mandate regarding structural design, materials, plumbing, or electrical systems that states what you can or cannot do when you build or remodel. Codes are intended to protect standards of health, safety, and land use.

Color Rendition Index (CRI): Measures the way a light source renders color. The higher the index number, the closer color resembles how it appears in sunlight.

Contemporary Style: A style of decoration or architecture that is modern and pertains to what is current.

Combing: A painting technique that involves using a small device with teeth or grooves over a wet painted surface to create a grained effect.

Correlated Color Temperature (CCT): Compares the warmth or coolness of light as it is produced, or the source as it appears to the viewer.

Dimmer Switch: A switch that can vary the intensity of the light source it controls.

Downlighting: A lighting technique that illuminates objects or areas from above.

Double-Hung Window: A window that consists of two framed-glass panels that slide open vertically, guided by a metal or wood track.

Duct: A tube or passage for venting indoor air to the outside.

Enclosure: Any material used to form a shower or tub stall, such as glass, glass block, or a tile wall.

Faux Painting: Various painting techniques that mimic wood, marble, and other stones.

Fittings: The plumbing devices that bring water to the fixtures. These can include shower heads, faucets, and spouts. Also pertcins to hardware and some accessories, such as towel racks and toilet-paper dispensers.

Fixture Spacing: Refers to how much space to include between ambient light fixtures for an even field of illumination.

Fixed Window: A window that cannot be opened. It is usually a decorative unit, such as a half-round or Palladian-style window.

Fixture: Any fixed part of the structural design, such as tubs, bidets, toilets, and lavatories.

Fluorescent Lamp : An energy-efficient light source made of a tube with an interior phosphorus coating that glows when energized by electricity.

Footcandle (Fc): A unit that is used to measure the brightness produced by a lamp. A footcandle is equal to one lumen per square foot of surface.

Form: The shape and structure of space or an object.

Full Bath: A bath that includes a toilet, lavatory, and bathing fixtures, such as a tub or shower.

Glass Block: Building blocks made of translucent glass used for non-load-bearing walls to allow passage of light. ▲

Glazing (walls): A technique for applying a thinned, tinted wash of translucent color to a dry undercoat of paint.

Ground Fault Circuit Interrupter (GFCI): A safety circuit breaker that compares the amount of current entering a receptacle with the amount leaving. If there is a discrepancy of 0.005 volt, the GFCI breaks the circuit in a fraction of a second. GFCIs are required by the National Electrical Code in areas that are subject to dampness.

Grout: A binder and filler applied in the joints between ceramic tile.

Halogen Bulb: A bulb filled with halogen gas, a substance that causes the particles of tungsten to be redeposited onto the tungsten filament. This process extends the lamp's life and also makes the light whiter and brighter.

Half Bath (powder room): A bathroom that contains only a toilet and a sink.

Highlight: The lightest tone in a room.

Incandescent Lamp: A bulb that contains a conductive filament through which current flows. The current reacts with an inert gas inside the bulb, which makes the filament glow.

Intensity: Strength of a color.

Jets: Nozzles installed behind the walls of tubs or showers that pump out pressurized streams of water.

Joist: Set in a parallel fashion, these framing members support the boards of a ceiling or a floor.

Lavatory or Lav: A fixed bowl or basin with running water and a drainpipe that is used for washing. A sink. ▲

Load-Bearing Wall: A wall that supports a structure's vertical load. Openings in any load-bearing wall must be reinforced to carry the live and dead weight of the structure's load.

Lumen: A term that refers to the intensity of light measured at a light source that is used for general or ambient lighting.

Muntins: Framing members of a window that divide the panes of glass.

Palette: A range of colors that complement each other.

Pedestal: A stand-alone lavatory with a basin and supporting column in one piece.

Pocket Door: A door that opens by sliding inside the wall, as opposed to a conventional door that opens into a room.

Pressure-Balancing Valve: Also known as a surge protector or antiscalding device. It is a control that prevents surges of hot or cold water in faucets by equalizing the amounts of hot and cold water that are pumped out at any time.

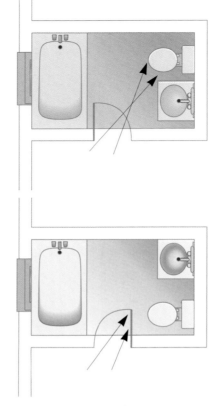

Scale: The size of a room or object.

Schematic: A detailed diagram of systems within a home.

Sconce: A decorative wall bracket that shields a bulb.

Sky Light: A framed opening in the roof that admits sunlight into the house. It can be covered with either a flat glass panel or a plastic dome.

Proportion: The relationship of one object to another.

Radiant Floor Heat: A type of hecting that is brought into a room via pipes that have been installed under the floor to carry hot water or electrical wire. As the hot water or electrical wire heats up, the flooring material warms and heat rises into the room.

Ragging: A painting technique that uses a crumbled piece of cloth to apply or remove small amounts of wet paint to create a pattern or texture.

Reflectance Levels: Refers to the amount of light that is reflected from a colored surface, such as a tile wall or painted surface. Some colors reflect light, others absorb it.

Roof Window: A horizontal window that is installed on the roof. Many are ventilating.

Sight Line: The natural line of sight the eye travels when looking into or around a room. ▲

Sliding Window: Similar to a double-hung window turned on its side. The glass panels slide horizontally.

Snap-In Grilles: Ready-made rectangular and diamond-pattern grilles that snap into a window sash and create the look of a true divided-light window.

Soffit: A boxed-in area just below the ceiling and above the vanity.

Space Reconfiguration: A term used to describe the reallocation of interior space without adding on.

Sponging: A paint technique that uses a small sponge to apply or remove small amounts of wet paint to create a pattern or texture on a surface.

Spout: The tube or pipe from which water gushes out of a faucet.

Stencil: A design cut out of plastic or cardboard. When paint is applied to the cut-out-area, the design will reproduce on a surface.

Stud: The vertical member of a frame wall, placed at both ends and usually every 16 inches on center. A stud provides structural framing and facilitates covering with drywall or plywood.

Subfloor: The flooring applied directly to the floor joists on top of which the finished floor rests.

Surround: The enclosure and area around a tub or shower. A surround may include steps and a platform, as well as the tub itself.

Task Lighting: Lighting designed to illuminate a particular task, such as shaving.

Tone: The degree of lightness or darkness of a color.

Traditional Style: A style of decoration or architecture that employs forms that have been repeated for generations without major changes.

Trompe L'Oeil: Literally means "fool the eye." A paint technique that creates a photographically real illusion of space or objects. ▼

True Divided-Light Window: A window composed of multiple glass panes that are divided by and held together by muntins.

Universal Design: Refers to products and designs that are easy to use by people of all ages and varying abilities.

Vanity: The countertop and cabinet used to support a sink. The vanity is usually included for storage purposes. It may double as a dressing table.

Whirlpool: A special tub that includes motorized jets behind the walls of the tub for water massages.

INDEX

PHOTO CREDITS

Cover *Photographer:* Nancy Hill. **p. 1** *Photographer:* David Livingston. **p. 2** *Photographer:* John Schwartz; *Designer:* Tess Guiliani for Ulrich, Inc. **p. 6** *Photographer:* Tria Giovan. **p. 8–11** *Photographer:* Nancy Hill. **p. 12** *Photographer:* Norman McGrath. **p. 13** *Photographer:* Tim Lee. **p. 14** *Photographer:* Mark Samu. **p. 15** *Photographer (top):* Jessie Walker. *Photographers (bottom):* Steve Gross and Susan Daley. **p. 16–17** *Photographer:* Norman McGrath. **p. 18** *Photographer (top):* Jessie Walker; *Photographer (bottom):* David Phelps. **p. 19** *Photographer:* Mark Samu, reprinted with permission from *House Beautiful Kitchens/Baths* © 1997 The Hearst Corporation. **p. 20–21** *Photographer:* David Livingston. **p. 22** *Photographer:* Melabee M Miller. **p. 23** *Photographer:* Jessie Walker; *Designer:* Blair Baby. **p. 24** *Photographer (top):* David Livingston. *Photographer (bottom):* Nancy Hill; *Architect:* Lloyd Jaevert. **p. 25** *Photographer:* George Ross; *Designer:* Patricia Bonis. **p. 26** *Photographer (top):* David Livingston. **p. 27** *Photographer:* Melabee M Miller; *Designer:* Pat McMillan. **p. 29** *Photographer:* Rob Melnychuk. **p. 31– 38** *Photographer:* David Livingston. **p. 42–43** *Photographer:* Mark Samu, reprinted with permission from *House Beautiful Kitchen/ Baths* ©1997 The Hearst Corporation; *Designer:* Carolyn Miller. **p. 44–46** *Photographer:* Rob Melnychuk. **p. 47** *Photographer:* Mark Samu, reprinted with permission *House Beautiful Kitchens/Baths* ©1998 The Hearst Corporation; *Architect:* Douglas S. Moyer. **p. 48** *Photographer:* Rob Melnychuk. **p. 55** *Photographer:* Melabee M Miller; *Designer:* Pat McMillan **p. 56–57** *Photographer:* Leonard Lammi; *Designer:* Cheryl Casey Ross. **p. 58** *Photographer (top, middle, and bottom):* Jessie Walker. **p. 59** *Photographer:* Mark Samu, re-printed with permission *House Beautiful Kitchens/Baths* ©1998 The Hearst Corporation; *Architect:* Douglas S. Moyer. **p. 60** *Photographer (top):* Mark Samu, reprinted with permission from *House Beautiful Kitchens/Baths*© 1997 The Hearst Corporation. *Photographer (bottom):* Philip Clayton-Thompson. **p. 61** *Photographer (top and bottom):* Mark Samu, reprinted with permission from *House Beautiful Kitchens/Baths* ©1997 The Hearst Corporation. **p. 62–63** *Photographer:* Jessie Walker; *Designer:* Blair and David Baby; *Architect:* Jim Landaker. **p. 64** *Photographer (top):* Jessie Walker; *Designer:* Claire Golan. *Photographer (bottom):* Jessie Walker; *Designer:* Claire Golan. **p. 65** *Photographer:* Melabee M Miller. **p. 66** *Photographer (top):* Carol Meyer; *Designer:* Virginia Burney. *Photographer (bottom):* Jessie Walker; *Designer:* Bauhs, Dring & Main, Ltd. **p. 67** *Photographer:* David Livingston. **p. 68–70** *Photographer:* Crandall & Crandall. **p. 71–72** *Photographer:* Scott Dorrance. **p. 74–75** *Photographer:* Peter Tata; *Architect:* Lawrence Speck. **p. 76** *Photographer:* Jennifer Deane. **p. 77** *Photographer:* Melabee M Miller. **p. 78** *Photographer:* Jennifer Deane. **p. 79** *Photographer (top):* Holly Stickley; *Designer:* George Tsconas. *Photographer (bottom):* Philip Clayton-Thompson. **p. 80** *Photographer:* Jessie Walker; *Designer:* Linda Brown, LaRue Creatives. **p. 81** *Photographer:* David Livingston. **p. 82** *Photographer (top):* Nancy Hill. *Photographer (bottom):* Melabee M Miller. **p. 83** *Photographer:* Holly Stickley. **p. 84–85** *Photographer (left):* Holly Stickley. *Photographer (right):* Leonard Lammi; *Designer:* Cheryl Casey Ross. **p. 86** *Photographer:* Jennifer Deane. **p. 87** *Photographer:* Philip Clayton-Thompson. **p. 88** *Photographer:* Holly Stickley. **p. 89** *Photographer:* Melabee M Miller. **p. 90–91** *Photographer:* David Livingston. **p. 92–93** *Photographer:* Jay Graham; *Designer:* Harrell Remodeling. **p. 94** *Photographer:* Jennifer Deane. **p. 95** *Photographer:* Peter Tata; *Architect:* Lawrence Speck. **p. 96–97** *Photographer:* Mark Samu, reprinted with permission from *House Beautiful Kitchen/ Baths* ©1998 The Hearst Corporation; *Designer:* Jeanne Leonard; *Architects:* Sears & Sears. **p. 98** *Photographer:* Mark Samu; *Designer:* Bruno Haase, The Tile Studio. **p. 99–101** *Photographer:* David Livingston. **p. 103** *Photographer:* David Livingston. **p. 104** *Photographer:* Melabee M Miller. **p. 106–107** *Photographer:* Holly Stickley. **p. 108** *Photographer:* David Livingston. **p. 109** *Photographer:* Mark Samu; *Designer:* Carolyn Miller. **p. 110** *Photographer:* Leonard Lammi; *Designer:* Cheryl Casey Ross. **p. 111** *Photographer:* Mark Samu; *Designer:* Lee Najman Designs. **p. 112–113** *Photographer:* David Livingston. **p. 114** *Photographer:* Mark Samu. **p. 115** *Photographer:* Nancy Hill. **p. 116–117** *Photographer:* Mark Lohman; *Designer:* Janet B. Lohman. **p. 117** *Photographer:* Philip Clayton-Thompson. **p. 118–120** *Photographer:* Nancy Hill. **p. 121** *Photographer:* David Livingston. **p. 122–123** *Photographer:* Jessie Walker. **p. 123** *Photographer:* Melabee M Miller. **p. 124** *Photographer:* Tria Giovan. **p. 125** *Photographer:* David Livingston. **p. 126** *Photographer:* Stephen Cridland. **p. 127** *Photographer:* David Livingston; *Designer:* Neil Kelly. **p. 130–134** *Photographer:* David Livingston; *Designers:* Joan Malter Osburn (pp. 130–133) and Lamperti Assoc. (p. 134). **p. 135** *Photographer:* Tria Giovan. **p. 136–137** *Photographer:* Nancy Hill. **p. 138** *Photographer:* Tria Giovan. **p. 139–140** *Photographer:* David Livingston. **p. 141** *Photographer:* Mark Samu. **p. 142** *Photographer:* Melabee M Miller. **p. 143** *Photographer:* Tria Giovan. **p. 144–145** *Photographer:* John Jensen; *Designer:* Luann Bauer. **p. 146–149** *Photographer:* David Livingston. **p. 150–151** *Photographer:* Tria Giovan. **p. 152** *Photographer:* Jessie Walker. **p. 153** *Photographer:* Mark Lohman; *Designer:* Janet B. Lohman. **p. 154** *Photographer:* David Livingston. **p. 155** *Photographer:* Jessie Walker. **p. 156** *Photographer:* Mark Lohman; *Designer:* Janet B. Lohman. **p. 157** *Photographer:* Philip Clayton-Thompson. **p. 158–161** *Photographer:* Rob Melnychuk. **p. 162** *Photographer:* Holly Stickley. **p. 166–168** *Photographer:* David Livingston. **p. 169** *Photographer:* Nancy Hill. **p. 170** *Photographer:* Leonard Lammi; *Designer:* Cheryl Casey Ross. **Back Cover** (clockwise) *Photographer:* David Livingston. *Photographer:* John Jensen; *Designer:* Luann Bauer. *Photographer:* Stephen Cridland.

SOURCES

Photographers

Philip Clayton-Thompson, Portland, OR; 503/234-4883. Crandall & Crandall, Dana Point, CA; 714/488-3222. Stephen Cridland, Portland, OR; 503/274-0954. Jennifer Deane, Naples, FL; 941/ 434-9000. Scott Dorrance, Cape Elizabeth, ME; 207/767-6512. Tria Giovan, New York, NY; 212/533-6612. Jay Graham, San Anselmo, CA; 415/459-3839. Nancy Hill, Pound Ridge, NY; 914/764-5859. John Jensen, Kensington, CA; 510/559-77565. Leonard Lammi, Cambria, CA; 805/ 927-3669. David Livingston, Mill Valley, CA; 415/383-0898, www.davidduncanlivingston.com. Mark Lohman, Los Angeles, CA; 213/933-3359. Rob Melnychuk, Vancouver, BC, CAN; 604/736-8066. Carol Meyer, Portland, OR; 503/777-0434. Melabee M Miller, Hillside, NJ; 908/527-9121. George Ross, Montclair, NJ; 973/744-5171. Mark Samu, Bayport, NY; 212/754-0415. John Schwartz, New York, NY; 212/567-9727. Holly Stickley, Tigard, OR; 503/639-4278. Peter Tata, Austin, TX; 512/320-0688. Jessie Walker, Glencoe, IL; 847/835-0522.

Bath Designers & Architects

Blair and David Baby, Wilmette, IL; 847/256-2527. Luann Bauer, San Francisco, CA; 415/621-7262. Bauhs, Dring & Main, Ltd. Chicago, IL; 312/649-9484. Patricia Bonis Interiors, Cresskill, NJ; 201/894-9082. Linda Brown, LaRue Creatives, Barrington, IL; 847/381-0979. Virginia Burney, Portland, OR; 503/223-1651. Claire Golan, Riverwoods, IL; 847/948-9294. Tess Guiliani, CKD, Ridgewood, NJ; 201/445-7302. Bruno Haase, The Tile Studio, Merrick, NY; 516/623-2600. Harrell Remodeling, Menlo Park, CA; 415/326-7093. Neil Kelly, Beaverton, OR; 503/288-NEIL. Carol R. Knott, A.S.I.D., Kenilworth, IL; 847-256-6676. Lamperti Assoc., San Rafael, CA; 415/454-1623. Jim Landaker, Deerfield, IL; 847/945-7975. Jeanne Leonard Interiors, West Hampton, NY; 516/288-7964. Janet Lohman, Los Angeles, CA; 310/471-3955. Carolyn Miller Interiors, Dix Hills, NY; 516/491-3010. Douglas S. Moyer, Sag Harbor, NY; 516/725-4878. Lee Najman Designs, Port Washington, NY; 516/944-7740. Joan Malter Osburn, San Francisco, CA; 415/487-2333. Cheryl Casey Ross, Cross Interiors, Van Nuys, CA; 818/988-2047. Sears & Sears, Quogue, NY; 516/653-4218. Ulrich, Inc., Ridgewood, NJ; 201/445-1260. Lawrence Speck, Austin, TX; 512/471-1922.

Have a home decorating, improvement, or gardening project? Look for these and other fine Creative Homeowner books wherever books are sold. . .

Projects to personalize your rooms with paint and paper. 300 color photos. 176 pp.; 9"×10"
BOOK #: 279723

Learn how to make the most of color. More than 150 color photos. 176 pp.; 9"×10"
BOOK #: 287264

How to create kitchen style like a pro. Over 150 color photographs. 176 pp.; 9"×10"
BOOK #: 279935

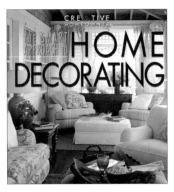

How to work with space, color, pattern, texture. Over 300 photos. 256 pp.; 9"×10"
BOOK #: 279667

Master stenciling, sponging, glazing, marbling, and more. Over 300 illustration. 272 pp., 9"×10"
BOOK #: 279550

Original ideas for decorating and organizing kids' rooms. Over 200 illustrations. 176 pp., 9"×10"
BOOK #: 279473

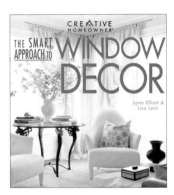

Design advice and industry tips for choosing window treatments. Over 225 illustrations. 176 pp., 9"×10"
BOOK # 279431

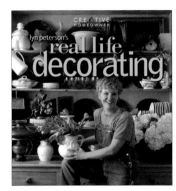

Interior designer Lyn Peterson's easy-to-live-with decorating ideas. Over 350 photos. 304 pp., 9"×10"
BOOK #: 279382

Complete houseplant guide. 200 readily available plants; more than 400 photos. 192 pp.; 9"×10"
BOOK #: 275243

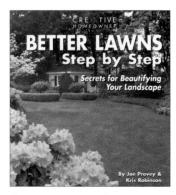

Create more beautiful, healthier, lower-maintenance lawns. Over 300 illustrations. 160 pp.; 9"×10"
BOOK #: 274359

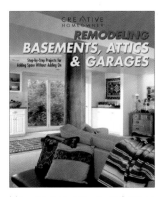

How to convert unused space into useful living area. 570 illustrations. 192 pp.; $8^1/2$"×$10^7/8$"
BOOK #: 277680

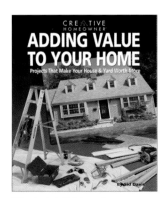

Filled with DIY projects to repair, upgrade, and add value. 500 illustrations. 176 pp.; $8^1/2$"×$10^7/8$"
BOOK #: 277006